A SOUTHERN LAWYER

A SOUTHERN LAWYER

Fifty Years at the Bar

BY
AUBREY LEE BROOKS

CHAPEL HILL
The University of North Carolina Press

© 1950 The University of North Carolina Press
All rights reserved
Library of Congress Catalog Card Number 50-10879
First printing, 1950
Second printing, 1983

To

MY WIFE

HELEN HIGBIE BROOKS

Contents

Chapter		Page
1	Plantation Boyhood	1
2	Some Things I Learned	10
3	Freshman at the Bar	16
4	Court Week in Roxboro	21
5	Politics in the Fifth District	28
6	Boyd & Brooks, Greensboro	33
7	Story of a Piedmont Town	40
8	Campaign of 1898—A Lucky Break	49
9	Schooling of a Prosecuting Attorney	53
10	Parting of the Ways	59
11	Plowing New Ground	64
12	The Gold Brick Case	70
13	Pass-Toters' Victory	74
14	Happenings at Court	78
15	A Political Misadventure	82
16	The Hour of Decision	88
17	A Lady, A Library, and A Lake	92

CHAPTER		PAGE
18	The Hartford of the South	96
19	Unusual Trials in Federal Courts	104
20	North Carolina Public Service Company v. Duke Power Company	113
21	From the Sublime to the Sordid	120
22	The Cole Case	127
23	Retribution in History	132
24	Roosevelt and the New Deal	136
25	Pleasure and Profit of Travel	143
26	The Cannon—Reynolds—Holman Case	149
27	The Lassiter Case and Others	160
28	Lawyer Becomes Litigant	167
29	The Romance of the Cigarette	188
30	Looking Backward	196
31	The Afternoon of Life	203
32	The Law's Final Decree	207
	Index	209

A SOUTHERN LAWYER

1

Plantation Boyhood

FATE made me a southerner, and Colonel William Byrd of Westover, Virginia, made me a North Carolinian. In 1728 the colonies of North Carolina and Virginia appointed a joint commission to survey and establish their dividing line, which had long been in dispute. Colonel Byrd headed the commission, which began its survey at the seacoast, continued westward through the Dismal Swamp, and ended in the meadows of the Dan River, not far west of what is now Danville, Virginia. The North Carolina commissioners abandoned the company when they reached Hyco River, because, as Colonel Byrd made clear in his classic *History of the Dividing Line,* the liquor gave out.

But this is where our story begins. The Hyco River at this point was to become the northernmost line of my father's plantation, and this made me at birth a Carolinian and not a Virginian.

May 21, 1871, was a fateful date for me. It was then that I came into a strange world, watched over at birth, I am told, by five grandmothers. When one stops to contemplate that through his veins courses the blood of innumerable ancestors—some good, some bad, and many indifferent—he can but wonder how it is possible to harmonize and direct the currents of inherited passions, prides, prejudices, vices, and virtues. Many men have struggled through life with these warring factions, sometimes one and sometimes another in the ascendency. I speak from experience, for I was a victim of this warring compound and complex.

My paternal grandfather, Larkin Brooks, was a thoroughgoing cavalier, while Andrew Hall, my grandfather on my mother's side, was a blue-stocking puritan. Grandfather Larkin Brooks, the cavalier, was a perfect prototype of the twentieth-century industrialist—adventurous and daring. He was six feet tall, weighed two hundred pounds, and was utterly fearless. He was among the first to build a tobacco factory in the state, many years before the Civil War. In the absence of railroad transportation, he used a fleet of horse-drawn wagons to haul manufactured plug tobacco to merchants in eastern North Carolina and South Carolina. He once went to Cincinnati, where he purchased a hundred head of horses and mules and led them on horseback to his home, a distance of over four hundred miles. This tremendous and difficult task was made possible by a queer quirk of animal nature. A drove of horses and mules will follow blindly the lead of a mare horse, wherever her rider takes them, without breaking ranks.

As a result of the war, Grandfather Brooks's slaves were freed, his business destroyed, and his fortune wrecked by surety obligations for his neighbors. I remember him as an impressive, loving old man, without health or money.

Grandfather Hall, the puritan, was the son of a Baptist minister and himself a minister of the Primitive Baptist church for fifty-six years. Three of his brothers were likewise ministers of the gospel. He lived in the spiritual world, caring nothing for earthly power and fame. His daily companions were the Bible and Whitefield's Sermons—his constant thought the eternal salvation of the soul; and he died as poor in worldly goods as the proverbial church mouse. He was six feet four inches tall, straight as an Indian, with black hair and a chin shaved like Lincoln's. He lived on a small farm, and his diversion, when not preaching the gospel, was hunting. He had a passion for it, which I inherited. In those days wild turkeys were abundant, and he told me that during his lifetime he had shot more than a thousand. When I was a stripling, too small to manage a horse alone, he frequently took me on these hunts, seated behind him astride a sheepskin across the rump of Talleyrand, his favorite saddle horse. When Fido, his trained turkey pointer, struck the trail of a drove of turkeys, he would race his horse to near the flush while I held on for dear life. He would become so absorbed and excited that when he dismounted from the horse to build a blind to shoot from, he forgot all about me, and his long leg as he swung it from the saddle would swipe me and the sheepskin to the ground at the horse's feet. But there was never any injury, for dear old Talleyrand knew perfectly well how to act his part.

It was a fascinating technique that followed. The old gentleman would quickly slash down a few saplings or leafy limbs and arrange them in a small circle to conceal our presence and that of the dog. Quiet restored, he would draw from his pocket a mechanism which he had arranged, known as a "turkey-caller." He could manipulate this yelper so as to imitate the call of a mother turkey hen as she always clucked to bring back near the flush her scattered offspring. It was great sport to see the handsome young gobblers come striding through the woods, responding to the perfect imitation of the mother hen's call.

The most unforgettable character of my childhood was my father's mother, Ann Brooks. She was society's dream of a queenly matron. The loss of property and slaves restricted her activities, but "Aunt Ann," as she was generally called, never lost an atom of her personal pride and dignity. She was always neatly and becomingly dressed, and presided over and directed the affairs of the household like one born to rule. Through kindness and consideration she retained the services of several former slaves, including a personal maid, who remained with her until her death. They continued to call her "Mistress" and did her bidding like obedient children. The memory of my childhood joy still lingers with me when, on my frequent visits, she took me to the corner cupboard and gave me cookies. The aroma from that corner cupboard when opened filled my soul with delight, and as I write these lines my olfactory nerves still do homage to a boy's recollection.

As I recall she was the most aristocratic looking woman I had ever seen. Her silvery gray hair was always becomingly arranged around a beautiful face, with sparkling eyes, which time had ennobled but cares had not hardened. She gave the impression of a charming mistress who had reigned over a household of pleasure and plenty in ante-bellum days, and was determined to preserve the tradition, though pleasure and plenty had vanished with the Lost Cause. My father, her firstborn, was the darling of her affections, and she was determined to give him a good education. In the last years of the war, in which he was too young to serve, she sent him to Tew's Military Academy at Hillsboro. After the close of the war, with the University of North Carolina closed, she inspired him to go to the University of Virginia, and thence to complete his medical course at Jefferson College in Philadelphia. How, with an invalid husband and the waste of war, she managed to finance his college attendance I never knew, but it stands as an example of what a high-minded, courageous mother can accomplish on a financial shoestring.

My father, Zachary Taylor Brooks, first read medicine under Dr. Harris, a noted practitioner of Halifax County, Virginia, before going to the University of Virginia. Later, at Jefferson College he was a member of the first graduating class after the war. He was a handsome man, medium-sized, with a striking personality that radiated charm and good humor. He had what is characterized by doctors as a good "bedside manner," and men and women have frequently said to me proudly, "Your father brought me into the world." With his training, his mentality, his personal charm and ambition, it would naturally be expected that he would locate in a thriving city, where his talents would be appreciated and his labors suitably rewarded. But an inconsiderate fate mastered him and, in the language of a North Carolina wag, he "made the wrong mistake" by returning to his birthplace and locating there, to practice in the economically exhausted neighborhood from which his improved talents offered the only certain avenue of escape. There was not a regular drugstore in the county; so he furnished his own apothecary shop, visited far and near, diagnosed patients' ailments, and furnished needed medicines, usually on promises to pay. In the following year he married his boyhood sweetheart, Chestina Hall, the only daughter of Andrew Hall, my puritan ancestor already described. A year later I came into the family, and fifteen months afterward a sister was born, but she did not live to womanhood.

Our home was situated on a high hill at the southern edge of a large oak forest. To the front, a mile away, loomed Indian Hill, embracing several miles of virgin timberlands abounding in game. It acquired its name from the Indian mounds and relics to be found there, a veritable treasure island for a boy.

I am glad that I was born on a plantation. I cannot imagine a more perfect place for a healthy boy to develop bone, muscle, character, and self-reliance, and to get acquainted with nature and nature's God. Our plantation in Person County extended to the banks of the Hyco River on the north and to Castle Creek on the west. The fertile valleys along these streams yielded corn and grass in abundance, while the uplands produced tobacco, wheat, and oats. One third of the boundary was in forest land, heavily timbered in oak, pine, hickory, and poplar. In these woods were squirrels, 'possums, and wild turkeys. In the springtime a wild gobbler occasionally ventured to visit the barnyard to pay court to domestic turkey hens, with the usual result of a bloody head battle, the home gobbler defending his harem from the prince of the forest.

When I was ten years old, my father gave me a beautiful, lemon-colored red bone hound pup. I named her Runwell, and she soon became the pet of the household, after my mother recovered from my having given the pup a saucer of milk in the best room in the house. For seven years, and until I left the plantation, she was to be my daily companion and playmate—the most admiring and slavish friend I ever had. In the years to follow, she repaid in every way the affection and care I bestowed upon her and failed me only once—but that is another story. There is magic in the memory of a boy's friendship for his dog, and there is solace in the memory of his dog's friendship for him. It is an unalloyed friendship, completely given, which is kind, which does not behave itself unseemly, and which never fails.

As Runwell grew to maturity, she became noted for her conformation, her endurance, and her speed. Her voice was rich and full like a bugle call. As we grew older, Runwell and I graduated from mere rabbit chasing to 'possum hunting at night. This required a companion who could wield an axe to cut down trees which the 'possum climbed to escape. I had a perfect companion for these adventures in John Hill, a robust Negro boy a few years my senior, the son of a tenant. For a country boy, a Negro boy chum and a good hound are the last word in human happiness. John and I were playmates—we fished and swam together in Hyco River, chased rabbits by day and hunted 'possums by night. If he ever had a different idea from mine, he never expressed it. He regarded me as perfect, and my esteem for him was but little less exalted.

As time passed, I became interested in fox hunting. The Bailey brothers, who lived in an adjoining community, had a crack pack of fox hounds, and, knowing Runwell's reputation as a fast-running hound, invited my father and me to bring her over and join in a chase. It was to be my first experience at fox hunting, and I have never forgotten my chagrin over the event. At the early crack of dawn, we loosed the hounds and followed them on horseback in search of Reynard. A gray fox was scented and put to running. He took a wide sweep, while we hurried down a plantation road to catch sight of the pack as it turned in our direction. On the cold, clear, crisp morning, the approaching orchestra of voices sounded like the strains of Sousa's Band. But, alas! I did not hear the ringing voice of Runwell. The fox crossed the road in sight of us, his bushy tail in the air, and the yelping pack, one hundred yards behind, sped by—but Runwell was not with them. Heartsick, I turned in my saddle, and, to my dismay, there stood Runwell at my horse's feet, with her tail between her legs. I tried in vain to hark her once more into the chase, but instead she looked up at me and, with her big brown eyes, seemed to say, "What is the meaning of all this? I have never seen or scented a fox before. I don't understand what all these strange hounds are trying to do, and I don't like it." Silently we trekked our way home, my father surprised, Runwell disgusted, and I struggling with my first great humiliation. But I did not lose faith in my dog.

By the next season, I accumulated a small pack of fox hounds and started out on my own. As soon as Runwell understood what I wanted her to do, she assumed her rightful place at the head of the pack, and the way she drove a fox was the envy of every hunter in the community. Tom Barnett, who lived about ten miles away, owned a pack that had the reputation of being the best in the county, and his lead hound, Plunger, was so fast, Barnett facetiously boasted, that when he was running with other packs it was necessary to tie a bell to his collar so that the other hounds could keep within hearing of him. Runwell and I were by now ready for a contest, and I invited Barnett over for a hunt. We had gray foxes in abundance that were usually good for a two-hour chase, but occasionally we came upon an old boar fox from a distance prospecting among the lady foxes. It was an ideal morning when Barnett arrived, and within a mile of the cast we came upon one of these visiting gentlemen, and the race was on. As is the custom of a wily old fox, he dodged and doubled back to the thick underbrush until he got a lead on the pack and then, in the language of my Negro chum, he "sold out" for home some eight miles away. The nature of the country was such and the get-away so quick and fast that all the horsemen were thrown out of the chase. Barnett and I rode in the general direction the pack had gone, inquiring along the way of farmers if they had seen the hounds. Imagine my thrill when in each instance the reply was, "Yes, they passed here about twenty minutes ago and a lemon-colored hound was leading them."

My father a few years later moved to Roxboro, the county seat, and we left my Negro boy chum, John Hill, on the farm. Two years later I was appalled to learn of his being sent to the State Penitentiary. It appeared that he was roaming the woods one Sunday when his fice dog came upon a turkey hen sitting on her nest, far away from any house. The dog killed the turkey and John carried it home. Someone reported him to the grand jury. He was arrested, tried without counsel, convicted of larceny, and sentenced to the State Penitentiary for two years. When I learned of it, I sought to help him, but was unable to locate him. He never came back, and neither his family nor I ever saw or heard from him again. Ten years later I became prosecuting attorney for the State, in a district comprising eight counties, and whenever a boy, white or black, came upon my docket, indicted for a first offense, he found in me an understanding friend, who sought to restore rather than to destroy—in memory of the hapless John Hill.

2

Some Things I Learned

THE fields and the forests, the streams, the birds and the wild flowers, all have a language of their own. Once a person is attuned to it, neither time nor place can ever erase its divine influence, nor rob him of the sweet memories which fix themselves upon a youthful mind and soul. There is a colloquialism which tersely puts it, "You can take a boy out of the country, but you can never take the country out of a boy." There is a good reason for this, because from his country rearing a boy learns things valuable to him in after life that he never forgets. Looking back across the generations, I still remember that down on the plantation in Person County, far removed from the conflicts and contests of urban life, I first learned from the streams that water always runs down hill and never runs back; I learned from the forests that its king, the white oak, sooner or later decays and dies; I learned that animals, when bred, always reproduce according to their kind; I learned from Mother Earth that the variations in the nature of the soil determine the character of the crops it produces, and that seed sown upon a rock will wither and die. The profoundest truth I learned from Mother Earth was that whatever a man sows, that shall he also reap. The experience and observation of three score and ten years have taught me that this truth is not confined to wild oats alone.

But the best teacher on the farm is the lowly mule. The sense and philosophy of the plantation mule, as an educator of the country boy who daily is associated with him at opposite ends of the plow, with only a plow line connecting the two, have been sadly overlooked. The abused mule comes into the world a bastard and an Ishmaelite, denied the pride of ancestry or even the hope of posterity. Yet, alike in peace and war, upon the plantation and on the battlefield, he has ever been man's most dependable servant. But it is as an instructor in the ways of life that the mule is a true educator of the boy who follows him. I still remember how my plow mules, Rhody and Jack, patiently plodded the furrow, day in and day out, obeying every order, until the noonday dinner bell at the home began to toll. They knew perfectly well this meant that dinner was to be served in the dining stalls, and they would stop to be unhitched. In some ways, a mule has more sense than a man. Hospitals, sanatoriums, and cemeteries are filled with smart men who did not know when to stop. Not so with the mule. Consider his ways, and you will find that when he is tired, no matter where he is at work he stops dead still, until he is rested; when he is overloaded he positively declines to pull; when urged to faster speed, he slows down before injuring his wind. No matter what is put before him, he never overeats, or drinks too much. In other words, he knows how to take care of his health, and in spite of hell and high water he does it. As a health conservationist he is a past master, and this has resulted in an old saying,

"Whoever saw a dead mule?" By contrast, in the human kingdom the cemeteries are full of prematurely dead jackasses.

Between school terms my task, like that of the sons of neighborhood farmers, was to make two blades grow where only one had grown before, but more particularly to guide a plow from sunup to sundown. Side by side with the hired hands, we cultivated and gathered the crops of corn, wheat, clover, and tobacco, while in the morning dawn and evening twilight I milked the cows and fed the hogs.

My father, from my earliest recollection, treated me as a companion, and as I grew up he shared with me his plans and hopes, and confided his cares and disappointments, which unhappily were many. My mother tutored me until I was ten, and then I entered Bethel Hill Academy, where my father had received his preparatory training. Grandfather Brooks had fostered the school before the Civil War and had selected as its first principal one of the Horner brothers, a noted educator of that period. The Academy was two miles away, and for six years, rain or shine, I trudged the muddy road back and forth, from September until May. There were no busses then to collect and carry children to and from schools, no gymnasium maintained at public expense to provide artificial exercise. The pampering and softening processes of educating youth were not then in vogue.

The school days at Bethel Hill were very happy ones, enlivened, as I grew into my teens, by an occasional puppy love, including, of course, a woman teacher as its object. I must confess a secret of this youthful romancing, which at sixteen did not end happily but did teach me my first lesson in sexology. Professor Hatcher, the old, dried-up-looking principal of the school, had his wife assist him in teaching. She was a lovely blonde, twenty years his junior, with eyes and figure that gave her a distinctly "come hither" look. She had what I have since learned is called sex appeal. She naturally loved admiration, and all the young bucks in school fawned upon her. So far so good, but when the trustees of the school came to electing a principal for another year, the rumor somehow got around that I had told Tom Gentry, a fellow student, that I had kissed her. This, of course, was shocking. I was petrified with fear lest my father and mother should hear of it. In despair, but with determination, I looked up Gentry and told him flatly that what I had said was that I believed I could kiss her. He grudgingly acquiesced, but the Hatchers moved on, and I drew in. I have made many mistakes in life, but from then on I understood it to be a crime to "kiss and tell." Years later I was to learn that a noted king had committed perjury like a gentleman when confronted with a delicate question affecting a lady's honor.

When General Johnston surrendered to General Sherman near Durham, North Carolina, just forty miles south of our plantation, the disbanded Union soldiers on their homeward trek spread over Person County like locusts, devouring as they went. My youthful mind was filled with the stories of how the Yankee soldiers had stolen my Grandfather Hall's horses and my Grandfather Brooks's manufactured smoking tobacco. Even to a boy who lived through the two decades of 1870 and 1880, humiliated by Reconstruction and poverty-stricken as the result of war, the thought of it was a nightmare. To add to our troubles, there were no railroads in this section to stimulate commerce, and the poor country roads were well-nigh impassable during the winter months.

A callow youth could hardly be expected to understand and appreciate the meaning and import of profound economic and social changes taking place around him. But in retrospect, as their consequences unfolded, memories are rekindled over the whys and wherefores, bringing back recollections that are tinged with sadness over the decay and disappearance of an old order, whose actors became the unhappy victims of forces beyond their control.

Halifax County, Virginia, which lay to the north and parallel with Person County, had been one of the old aristocratic counties of Virginia. The F.F.V.'s flourished there, with their broad and fertile acres, slaves in abundance, and colonial mansions for the abode of a well-bred and cultured people. Appomattox ended their economic world, and with its ending, there followed the gradual decay of the social structure which leisure and means had so plentifully maintained. We of the following generation were to get the backwash of all this at full tide.

But boy and girl were quite unmindful of Time's old problems or of comparative poverty—and Hyco River was no bar to my weekend visits to those once lordly old homes and the lovely young girls who were bravely trying to preserve a tradition. Among the notables of those families were the Faulkners, Hunts, Owenses, Glenns, Bruces, Harrises, and Gardners.

The physical appearance of these places was one of an elegant decay that still haunts me. The yard fences had rotted and fallen away in sections; the outhouses, barns, and stables showed the ravages of time; and the lawns had grown up in weeds and bushes. The abundant English boxwood was the only landmark that had defied the years and, with age, had grown more beautiful. The Manor House still stood, but weather had robbed it of its paint; here and there a window blind or a window pane was missing, the roof was patched, the colonial columns looked infirm and uncertain of their footings, and the worn porch floors suggested that the visitor should watch his step.

Once you entered the spacious hall with its high ceiling and its winding stairway and mahogany rail looming in the background, you instantly became intoxicated with an indescribable atmosphere of faded splendor. On one side of the hall was the spacious drawing room, furnished with priceless antiques—there could be no doubt of their antiquity. In one end of the room was the tuneless piano. The damask and horsehair coverings of the sofas, settees, and chairs had suffered from use until the stuffing beneath was visibly seeking to escape. The carpet showed signs of footsteps and the only way to see what was its original pattern was to look under the piano. But in the dining room you were brought face to face with old age and youth, with the elegance of the past and the meagerness of the present, with a glory that had died and a beautiful youth that was denied social expression by the proscriptions of class and by environment and lack of opportunity. The Chippendale mahogany sideboard and chairs to match were mute reminders of a luxury that had gone from this household. Even the monogrammed silver tableware, through long use, had lost its largeness and lustre .

But, like Moore's observation, "You may break, you may shatter the vase if you will, But the scent of the roses will hang 'round it still," the spirit and charm of these old homes was still in flower in the lovely daughters. Remoteness from good schools and poverty had denied them a finished education and the opportunity to travel—and what was worse, their brothers had been forced to seek other fields, while only the sons of overseers and tenants remained from among whom they might choose mates. Preserving their social and class integrity, they grew up like American Beauty roses, with all the grace and beauty of their ancestors—but alas, most of them to fade in a social and economic desert of ineligible swains.

At seventeen I was interested only in the girls, basked in their smiles, and was enthralled by their beauty. In the very nature of things, this was all that I could do about it.

3

Freshman at the Bar

IT WAS seemingly an unkind fate that brought a carefree country-loving boy of seventeen face to face with a condition that was to change the entire course of his life. My mother, who for several years had been a semi-invalid, watched over me like a guardian angel. Her constant admonition was that I must, at whatever sacrifice, acquire a college education. But that took money, and we had no money. The family's situation was common to all southerners, in the dreadful eighties, who tilled the soil. The tragedy of it was that surplus cash could not be gotten from the products of the farm at the prices then prevailing. Tobacco was the only cash crop, and year after year it sold on the market for seven dollars per hundred. Wheat and corn brought forty cents a bushel, chickens twenty cents apiece, eggs six cents a dozen, and so on.

To those families like my father's, who had once owned slaves and were not accustomed to manual labor, the situation was hopeless. My father had undertaken to supplement his small income from the practice of medicine by operating the farm with hired labor. This form of absentee-landlordism did not pay then, and never has since, even with good prices for crops; but it did serve to divide his energies. He was the world's worst bill collector, and so he lost going and coming. Under such pressure and disappointments, his health became impaired. With my mother an invalid also, the future looked to me as dark as midnight, and I realized there was nothing I could do to improve it.

But my mother never faltered in her solicitude for my escape from a combination of realities that had baffled my father and had apparently closed the door of hope against her son. None of my family on either side had ever been a lawyer, but for some unaccountable reason I was consumed with an ambition to become one. In after years I was reminded that the reason I gave to my associates at the time for such a decision was that, as a lawyer, I could sleep late in the morning. In the country it was considered a virtue to go to bed with the chickens and to be up before sunrise, but to me it was a vice.

Determined to try my own wings at seventeen, I secured a license from the county superintendent of public instruction to teach in a common school, and in the fall of 1888 I began in a one-room free school, two miles from home, at the munificent salary of thirty-five dollars a month. A number of the pupils had been students with me six months before at the Bethel Hill Academy, and several were my seniors.

Having thus escaped from the drudgery of the plantation, I resolved not to return to it. After many family conferences my father, in 1890, decided to move to Roxboro, county seat of Person County, where a railroad had just been completed. After teaching another year in the public schools at the increased salary of forty dollars a month, I accumulated enough cash to enter the University of North Carolina. A serious attack of typhoid fever prevented my finishing the college course. I next turned to a business course at the University of Kentucky. But the law kept calling, and I re-entered the University of North Carolina and finished the law course in September, 1893.

With this meager preparation and no money, I returned to Roxboro, a village of eight hundred people, to engage in the great adventure. Colonel Charles S. Winstead, the dean of the bar, took me in as a partner, just why I never knew, except that at seventy his time was taken up with his farming interests and banking, and little attention was paid to the small law business that came to his office.

In Person County the Superior Court convened for the trial of cases only three times a year, each a one-week term. There were no manufacturing industries in the county and no litigation of importance except criminal cases, appeals from the justice of the peace, and an occasional dispute over the title to a farm. Since there was scarcely any office work for the seven lawyers at the bar, the principal diversion was trying petty cases before Squire Newton, the justice of the peace. He held his court in the county courthouse, which gave added dignity to His Honor's dispensing of justice.

Great contests some of these were, often lasting for several hours, during which the lawyers displayed their learning (or lack of it) and their oratorical powers. The Judge, when announcing his decision, would always take pains to give as a reason for it some point that had not been made by counsel on either side. This was to impress the audience which usually attended these hearings with his superior knowledge of the law. My cash receipts for the first year amounted to the grand total of $265. Boarding and lodging with my parents was all that saved me that year.

A few years before, there had come to the Roxboro bar W. W. Kitchin, who was greatly to influence my life and political thinking. He had lent me a copy of Blackstone's *Commentaries* while I was teaching school and had directed my first studies in the law. He was a member of the famous Kitchin family of Halifax County. His father, "Buck" Kitchin, had been a member of Congress, and he, in 1896, was to be elected a member of Congress and later governor of North Carolina. His brother, Claude Kitchin, was to win a national reputation as chairman of the powerful Ways and Means Committee of the House of Representatives during the Wilson administration. Will Kitchin, as he was familiarly called, was one of the handsomest young men in the state, and, I think, the most effective political debater I ever heard. He had a spotless character, a vigorous mind, a winning personality, and the tongue of a great orator. It was inevitable that I, a freshman at the bar enjoying his personal friendship, should become his understudy and ardent follower. Under his influence I was promptly to grow my political pinfeathers—and as suddenly to lose them. Kitchin was chairman of the County Democratic Executive Committee, and when the convention of the senatorial district, composed of Person and Granville counties, met at Berea, in July, 1894, to nominate a Democratic candidate for the State Legislature he had me nominated for the State Senate. When told of the unexpected honor I was naturally elated, but I was soon reminded that the State Constitution required a senator to be twenty-five years old, and I was only twenty-three. I declined the nomination, and thus ended my first lesson in politics.

During the campaign that fall, Kitchin and I traveled by horse and buggy to fill political speaking engagements in Person, Orange, Granville, Caswell, and Durham counties. On these tours we occasionally spent the night at some farmer's home, and slept in the same bed. I furnished the horse and buggy, which belonged to my father, and Kitchin furnished the oratory. He encouraged and coached me to make stump speeches for the Democratic party. My political textbook was the *Congressional Record,* from which I culled choice bits of florid flights of eloquence, praising the Democratic party and its founder, Jefferson, on the one hand, and, on the other, picturing the sins of the Republican party. The farmers generally were Democrats, and we were in the Bible Belt, where the Baptists predominated, and Kitchin, a distinguished brother in the faith, was their beau ideal.

4

Court Week in Roxboro

WHEN I came to the bar, North Carolina was divided into twelve judicial districts with each district nominating a Superior Court judge, and a solicitor who was the prosecuting attorney for the State in each district. The judges were elected by the State at large and rotated from one district to another, presiding six months in each district before moving on to the next. North and South Carolina are the only states in the Union that still retain this rotating system. Most of the counties composing these districts were rural, and usually a few weeks of court a year were all that were needed to dispose of the civil and criminal cases over which these courts had exclusive jurisdiction.

Person County, as already stated, had three one-week terms, which convened respectively in April, August, and November each year. There were no hard-surfaced roads or automobiles to facilitate intercourse among the people of the county, and so court week, by custom, became the most important event in their lives. They could meet each other, take a look at the new judge, hear his charge to the jury, exchange views, swap lies and horses, drink good liquor (which was plentiful), and occasionally raise a little hell on the side. The big day of these courts was Tuesday, when every man in the county, old and young alike, who could, quit business and attended court. During its sessions the courtroom was packed with interested spectators who enjoyed the tilts between the lawyers and the occasional embarrassment of witnesses by vigorous cross-examinations.

The courthouse, as was the custom, was built in the main square of the town with the lawyers' one-story offices fronting on the court green. During the intermission of court, gayety and entertainment were provided by patent medicine vendors who had a cure for everything. "Cheap John," as he was called, had for public sale shelf-worn clothes and various trinkets which, he vociferously asserted, were the greatest bargains on earth. On another section of the square was a stand where ginger cakes and cider were sold. Some distance removed, on vacant lots, the horse traders gathered to swap their plugs, and sometimes good-looking horses, but in nearly every instance the horse or mule was either spavined or wind-broken or, on account of age, was a prospect for the bone yard. In this arena it is safe to say that more lies were told per minute, extolling the merits of the animals, than on any other occasion in the bounds of the state. These performances lasted throughout the day, not diverted or disturbed by the sittings of the court.

An unforgettable character in Roxboro, in the thick of all this, was Dan Andrews, proprietor of the principal saloon in the village. His flashy attire in itself bordered on assault and battery. In court week he would rig himself up with a blood-red vest adorned with brass buttons, a Prince Albert coat, and a cowboy sombrero hat. When an occasional patron of his saloon would get too drunk to navigate he would throw him out, and now and then he would be indicted. His case was then tried before a justice of the peace but he never employed counsel. A young limb of the law once asked him why he never hired a lawyer to defend him. He replied, "I have found that it is cheaper and safer to hire witnesses." He pulled another stunt one day when a Turk and his bear were entertaining the crowd. The bear was being put through his tricks for the amusement of the spectators and in consideration of such voluntary contributions as might be dropped into his cup. Dan Andrews created a sensation by giving the Turk and the bear each a mug of beer dashed with croton oil.

One of the most sensational trials, one filled with drama and pathos, occurred in Roxboro in 1895. Nathan Lunsford, one of the older members of the bar, lived on his plantation in the country eight miles distant. He affected to be an infidel, though he was a very kindly and upright man. He was among the first in the county to buy a bicycle, which he rode to and from his home to the county seat. On account of the bad condition of the highway he would ride his bicycle along bypaths to avoid the mud, and in doing so he crossed the plantation of his neighbor, Mr. Moore, who was a very devout Methodist and had a great contempt for his infidel neighbor. Moore indicted Lunsford for trespass, and the justice of the peace before whom the case was tried found Lunsford guilty and fined him one dollar. He appealed from the conviction to the Superior Court and employed W. W. Kitchin and myself to defend him. W. P. Bynum, an able lawyer, was the solicitor for the State, but to make certain of a conviction, Mr. Moore employed J. S. Merritt, one of the leaders of the local bar, and R. B. Boone and Victor S. Bryant, two distinguished trial lawyers from the adjoining county of Durham.

Lunsford's contention was that the wagon way he was traversing had been long used by the public as a mill road and on that account had become dedicated to a public use. This opened up a great field of ancient law and afforded an opportunity for counsel on both sides to delve into rusty law books and quote authorities pro and con for their respective contentions. The trial in the Superior Court lasted three days, and the jury, after sleeping over the matter one night, rendered a verdict of guilty.

Before sentence was imposed, Lunsford approached me with the request that I make a motion to set aside the verdict because he had been reliably informed that Bynum, the solicitor for the State, while the jurors were engaged in trying to reach a verdict, took the foreman of the jury, Gabriel Neal, to his room at the hotel and gave him a drink of whiskey and that Neal speaking for the jury the next day had rendered the verdict of guilty. I suggested that Kitchin should make the motion as he was his senior counsel, to which Lunsford replied that Kitchin had said that the juror Neal was an honorable man, that he did not believe the solicitor intended any wrong or that giving the juror a drink had influenced his verdict, and that he would not make such a motion. "If neither of you will act," said Lunsford, "I will make the motion myself and support it with my own affidavit."

Everyone concerned, the judge and the lawyers on both sides, realized that there was dynamite in the proposition and that an explosion was likely to follow. The presiding judge, Coble, was a kindly man, but rather timid, and he avoided the issue until the closing hours of court on Saturday. When he called the case for judgment, Lunsford arose and announced that he wished to make a motion in the case to set aside the verdict. The Judge stated to him that he hesitated to entertain the motion because it was being made by the defendant; that he was represented by counsel of record who were then present in court; and that they were the proper ones to present whatever motion was to be made.

To this Lunsford replied, "Your Honor, I did have counsel in the trial of the case but since my conviction they have deserted me and have declined to make this motion. The defendant in this case, Nathan Lunsford, is a client of mine and I demand the right to speak for him."

The court allowed him to proceed with the reading of his affidavit in support of the motion. The gravamen of the affidavit was that while the jury was considering his case, and before they had rendered their verdict, the solicitor for the State took the foreman of the jury to his room and drank him at the public expense; that such conduct was contrary to the ethics and the proper procedure of the administration of justice; and that the verdict on this account should be set aside. Technically, we all knew that the undisputed facts gave definite merit to his motion. It would have made an interesting moving picture scene —the dejected and embarrassed expressions on the face of Lunsford's counsel, whom he accused of having deserted him, and on the faces of the solicitor and his associates, who sat mute. Then followed an argument, brief but one of the most dramatic I have ever listened to.

"May it please the court," said Lunsford, "I apologize for appearing before this court but the necessity of the occasion demands it. I am embarrassed because my practice of the law has been confined almost exclusively to appearance before justices of the peace and the probate judge. I did not have the opportunity of acquiring an education as did the solicitor for the State and his associates, and my late counsel. I did not begin the study of law until I was married and had a family of children. The little law that I learned was at night by the flame of lightwood knots while my children were playing around the room. I call to Your Honor's attention that the solicitor for the State in his argument to the jury, in order to induce a verdict in his favor, said that I was a lawyer and knowing the law was the more guilty for its violation. By the same logic, Your Honor, the solicitor for the State, who comes of a distinguished family, is highly educated and has been honored on account of his learning by the people of the district as its chief prosecuting attorney. He, therefore, better than I, knew the law; and applying the same rule to him, when he took the foreman of the jury, while it had in its keeping my guilt or innocence, to his room and drank him at the public expense, I submit that he is the more guilty of the two." He then reminded the court that the associate counsel, employed to aid the solicitor in the prosecution, had each in their arguments to the jury referred to him as the "Mogul of Shakerag" and the "King of Shakerag" (this was the designation commonly applied to the community in which he lived), whose rights no one dared dispute. Turning upon them he said: "To this quartet I throw down the gage of war; lay on, Macduff, and damned be him that first cries, Hold!, enough!" As a climax he dramatically exclaimed to the Judge, "If this course of conduct shall be approved and receive the sanction of this court, well may the sheriff in opening and closing our court say, 'God save the State and this honorable Court.'" The verdict, of course, was set aside and that ended the case.

It was the custom of the court to charge the jury upon convening of court, and then direct the sheriff to notify the solicitor that the court was ready for him. When the solicitor appeared in court he strode down the aisle, and all eyes were turned upon him in solemn silence. He, to them, represented the majesty of the law and the power of the State. Solicitor Bynum—big, handsome and imposing looking—took his seat at the prosecutor's table. I looked with admiration at him and thought if I could ever hold such a position I would be supremely happy, little dreaming that in three years I would be his successor.

Landsdale, the clerk of the court, was a retired Baptist preacher—an interesting old man with a quaint sense of humor. He told of a young man, Tapp, who had gone from the county to Wake Forest College, studied for the ministry, and applied to a country church in eastern North Carolina for a position as minister. He gave Brother Landsdale as a reference and the church asked about Tapp's qualifications. Replying, Landsdale wrote the brethren that he knew Brother Tapp very well, that he was a man of good character, but, in the first place he had a poor delivery, and in the second place he had nothing to deliver.

One August afternoon after adjournment of court, I invited the judge and the clerk to go driving with me. The judge, who hailed from Asheville, had a glass eye and was telling us how wonderful it was; that it fitted perfectly and looked so much like the other eye that a casual observer would not notice that he had an artificial eye. After he had expanded on the merits of the eye, old man Landsdale said: "Judge, can you see as good out of that eye as you can the other?"

5

Politics in the Fifth District

IN THE years following the Civil War, most of the farmers of North Carolina became ardent Democrats; but starvation prices for farm products, which obtained in the eighties and early nineties, caused an economic debacle throughout the South and resulted in the farmers' organizing granges and alliances, leaving the Democratic party and joining the Populist party as a revolt against the existing political order. In North Carolina (as in many other states) a fusion occurred between the Populist and Republican parties, which gave their combined forces political control of the state and local governments. Person County was in the fifth North Carolina congressional district which, as a result of this political alliance, had elected Tom Settle (Republican), a representative to Congress. The Populists had charged to the account of Grover Cleveland most of their ills, and when the Democratic party repudiated his leadership and in 1896 nominated Bryan for president, the tide of revolt from the Democratic party began to recede. Bryan's famous speech, delivered at the Democratic National Convention in Chicago, had aroused the populace of the nation and offered a ray of hope to the forgotten man. It is doubtful if any other single speech in the history of this nation ever influenced so many people, and particularly the matchless phrase denouncing the gold standard, "You shall not press down upon the brow of labor this crown of thorns; you shall not crucify mankind upon a cross of gold."

Into this political maelstrom W. W. Kitchin dared to go, announcing his candidacy for Congress against Settle. The Democratic Congressional Convention met in Greensboro, and Kitchin asked me to nominate him. I placed his name before the convention; he was nominated by acclamation since it was thought to be an empty honor, and the convention nominated me for presidential elector. Kitchin challenged Settle to a joint discussion throughout the district, and this resulted in one of the most celebrated political contests the state has ever witnessed. Both men were young, Kitchin thirty and Settle thirty-six; and both were scions of distinguished fathers who had won fame in the political life of the state. Settle's father, for whom he was named, had been a justice of the Supreme Court and was renowned for his brilliant debate with the immortal Zebulon B. Vance in 1876 in their canvass for governor. Kitchin's father had been a member of Congress from the third district and was recognized as a forensic campaigner.

Tom Settle and Will Kitchin, as they were familiarly known, were both strikingly handsome; they were well educated, and possessed charming manners. Settle had already demonstrated his political acumen and versatility as a debater by having twice won the election to Congress in a normally Democratic district.

Soon after their debates began, it became apparent that Kitchin was a worthy foe for the great Settle and that a man's-size fight was on. News spread that a thrilling contest was being waged in the old fifth district, and crowds from far and near came to hear their debates. Each engagement demonstrated that Settle at last had met his match and that Kitchin's logic and oratory were winning votes away from him. As the canvass progressed, the eyes of the entire state looked with keenest interest to the outcome, hoping that the Democrats might win one congressional seat, and fearing that the North Carolina delegation would be solidly Republican. Kitchin won by a small majority and for the next two years was the only Democratic member from the Old North State in either branch of Congress.

Settle's defeat was induced largely by his bold defense of the gold standard and his unsuccessful attempt to ridicule the advocates of free silver, which included the Populists. One of his wisecracks about the Populist strength is still quoted—that "they had done more business on the capital invested than any similar organization in the history of the nation." As presidential elector and friend of Kitchin, I made speeches all over the district in an effort to pour water on his political wheel, and extolled the virtues of free silver, Bryan, and the regenerated Democratic party. The enthusiasm and abandon of youth made up in part for my ignorance on the money issue, but after three score and ten years I still observe many ignoramuses in high places descanting on this subject with an equal lack of intelligence.

These experiences were to prove valuable to me in many ways that I did not then anticipate. It enlarged my acquaintance to include the political leaders in the most populous district in the state, and gave me an opportunity to develop the technique of public speaking to mixed and sometimes large audiences, to array my arguments and to play upon their political ardor, passions, and prejudices as was the custom of the times. As my horizon broadened a new vista appeared, inviting me to wider fields of endeavor, particularly in politics.

Under the tutelage of Kitchin, the glamour of Bryan, and the magic and saving grace of the free and unlimited coinage of silver at the ratio of sixteen to one, I became active in the political arena. Kitchin and I attended the Democratic State Convention held in Raleigh in 1896 to nominate a governor and a state ticket. Several candidates were mentioned for governor, but the convention was overwhelmingly in favor of drafting Walter Clark, who had been unanimously elected to the Supreme Court bench in 1894 through the support of each of the political parties. Clark felt that he could not afford, under the circumstances, to quit the bench; so the convention endorsed him for vice president of the United States and directed that his name be presented to the National Democratic Convention soon to meet in Chicago. The State Convention nominated Cyrus B. Watson, a distinguished lawyer and Confederate veteran from Winston-Salem. He made a brilliant campaign, but in a three-cornered fight with Daniel L. Russell, the Republican nominee, and Major William A. Guthrie, the Populist nominee, he failed of election by only a few thousand votes.

Among his other engaging qualities, Watson was a great humorist, and one of the stories he delighted to repeat was an experience he had during his canvass for governor in one of the extreme mountain counties. It was on a Tuesday of court when he was billed to deliver an address during the intermission. Sitting on the veranda of the country town hotel his attention was attracted to a flashily dressed man sitting near him. He remarked to the stranger that there seemed to be a much larger crowd gathered than was customary even on Tuesday of court. The man replied, "You didn't know that a sensational case is to be tried here this afternoon." Watson inquired, "What is the nature of the case?" The man enthusiastically replied, "A man has been indicted and is to be tried for buggery," and pointing his finger to himself he added, "I am the gentleman who was buggered."

Watson was essentially a man of the soil. Born and reared on a farm, he knew the farmers' hopes and aspirations. He developed into one of the state's greatest trial lawyers. He rode the circuit with the judges and after court would entertain the crowd with his lively stories gathered from the people in Stokes, Surry, Yadkin, Davie, and other western counties.

All through that section of the state the roads were poor and there were few newspapers. The churches thus became centers for the exchange of community news. One of Watson's prize stories dealt with this. An old brother reported to the pastor that he had lost a heifer and wanted him to announce it at Sunday's meeting. After the minister had delivered his sermon, he announced to the congregation that Sister Smith, the organist, was soon to be married and that he felt it would be a nice thing for the church to get up a purse for her. The old farmer who was sitting in the congregation and was a little deaf, thought the preacher was talking about his heifer. At this point he arose and said, "Parson, you neglected to tell them that she has three teats and a black spot on her belly."

Soon after Watson's campaign for governor, he was employed by the plaintiff in the famous case of *Gattis* v. *Kilgo*. One of his sallies in that case has become a classic. Kilgo was president of Trinity College and the Dukes were interested in the suit. On the gateway to the entrance of Trinity College was the inscription: "Eruditio et Religio." Watson, in his argument to the jury, said it should be changed to read: "Eruditio et Religio et Cigaretto et Duko."

6

Boyd & Brooks, Greensboro

BY 1897 I realized that the limited demands for legal services in my home county could not adequately support the eight lawyers at the bar. While my practice had grown, it still returned less than a thousand dollars a year, and in the meantime I had married, in 1895, Miss Maud Harris of Reidsville, under the fatuous belief that two could live as cheaply as one. Our living with my father happily concealed the fallacy of that belief and solved the problem for me, but future prospects were uninviting.

It was a strange and unpredictable set of circumstances that took me from Roxboro to Greensboro to live. There had long existed a tradition among the members of the bar and bench that Greensboro was the most attractive place in the state to practice law. It was a railroad center located on the main line of the Southern, connecting with the North through Washington and with the deep South through Atlanta. It was here that the United States judge for the Western District of North Carolina resided and held court. Its bar enjoyed a distinguished reputation and the services of its members were sought after throughout the state. But from the village of Roxboro to this expanding metropolis seemed a far cry.

This is how the transition occurred. My partner, Colonel Charles S. Winstead, had been United States collector of internal revenue under President Grant and during these years had lived in Greensboro, where he formed an intimate friendship with another distinguished Republican lawyer, Colonel James E. Boyd, who enjoyed a remunerative practice in both the Federal and state courts. One day Colonel Winstead sent me to Greensboro to secure a restraining order from the presiding judge. Because of my inexperience—this was my first experience in such a case—he suggested that I call on his friend Colonel Boyd to assist, and gave me a letter of introduction.

Colonel Boyd was very gracious and after I had secured the order he invited me to visit with him in his office. During the conversation I casually remarked that I would like to practice law in Greensboro. To my surprise he told me that President McKinley had promised to make him an assistant to the attorney general of the United States; that when the appointment came he would be glad to take me in as a partner to look after the office while he was in Washington. Three months later on May 7, 1897, a note came from him saying that he was leaving soon for Washington and asking me to come up and take over. Few things in life have ever elated me more than the appearance of the partnership name of Boyd & Brooks over the doorway of *our* office.

There were few stenographers in those days and I soon found that Colonel Boyd disliked details. Our partnership arrangement extended only to new matters coming into the office, but Colonel Boyd had a number of pending cases for trial in which I soon observed he had made little preparation. Trying to make myself useful, I took the pleadings in these cases, drafted the issues to be submitted to the jury, and prepared a short brief of the law in each case. This resulted in my being invited to take part in the trial of the cases, and Judge Boyd was very generous in giving me a portion of the fees.

In Guilford County, one of the largest and richest counties in the state, frequent terms of the Superior Court were necessary in order to dispose of the large volume of business that arose. Under the reflected reputation of Colonel Boyd, notwithstanding my youth, business continued to come to the office, which gave me much needed experience, a general acquaintance, and a better income.

I was soon to receive a shock and a challenge. One day Colonel McIntosh, a distinguished-looking ante-bellum lawyer walked into the office with this declaration: "I am the general counsel of the Postal Telegraph Company throughout the South. My business here is to institute a condemnation proceeding against the Southern Railway to obtain leave to construct our telegraph poles and lines along its right of way throughout North Carolina. I don't know any lawyers here, but in walking around the court green this morning I observed the name of Boyd & Brooks, Attorneys. My home is in Mississippi, where one of the dearest friends I have is named Brooks, and I decided to come in and engage you to represent us simply on account of your name."

It took all the nerve I ever possessed and all the assurance anyone ever accused me of to undertake this job. What I didn't know about the method of procedure or the law applicable to such a case would have filled a volume. We decided, with emphasis on the *we,* to institute a proceeding before the clerk of the Superior Court of Guilford County asking for the condemnation of an easement along the railroad's right of way and for the appointment of commissions to assess the damages. The Western Union Telegraph Company, which already had lines along the Southern Railway System, did not want any competition, and soon there appeared a distinguished battery of lawyers from Richmond, Virginia, representing the Western Union, which filed a petition in the United States District Court and had the case removed to that tribunal for disposition. My troubles were multiplied and my embarrassment increased from the fact that there was no United States statutory law governing such a proceeding. After prolonged litigation, which went to the United States Circuit Court of Appeals, we succeeded in securing the right of way, and for nominal damages, as the court held that since the Southern Railway's right of way had been acquired for public use it could not recover damages from the Postal Company, as this was also for a public use and did not interfere with the operation of the railroad.

The partnership of Boyd & Brooks continued for five years, until Colonel Boyd was appointed to the Federal bench. During McKinley's administration a vacancy occurred in the office of judge of the Federal District for Western North Carolina, and the President appointed Colonel Boyd to this position. Boyd was a handsome man, a loyal Republican, with a quick mind and good courtroom manners. I was sure that he would make an honest upright judge, and this gave me an opportunity, when his name was presented by President McKinley, to do him a real service by personally enlisting the support of the leading Democratic lawyers of my district and in other parts of the state. During Judge Boyd's long tenure of office, he never forgot this kindness, and I still remember his gracious help to me before I was able to make my way alone.

In those days judges and lawyers alike loved to linger over

the bottle and tell rich and racy stories. Boyd was a prince at such parties and his taste for the ladies was not less acute than his taste for good liquor.

He had a good sense of humor, which is illustrated by a story he often repeated on himself. Statesville was one of the towns in which he held court, and Henry Clay Cowles was the clerk of his court, at whose home he stayed while holding court there. He arrived one Monday from Washington, where he had spent the previous weekend enjoying himself. At breakfast he declined to eat any of Mrs. Cowles's fried chicken or country ham, saying that his stomach was out of order. She then suggested waffles, sourwood honey, and country-made butter. When he declined all of these, the Cowles's precocious ten-year-old boy, who was at the table, couldn't stand it any longer and blurted out, "Mama, maybe the darned old fool can eat a raw egg."

A favorite story among the members of the bar occurred in Sampson County Court, where Judge R. B. Peebles, a learned but stern judge, was holding court. Suit was being tried in an action for $1,000 claimed to be due on a fertilizer bill. The facts disclosed that the plaintiff, who was a horse-trader and dealer in fertilizer, had a bill against a tenant of a retired Presbyterian minister. The minister was an old man, crippled by rheumatism, and much beloved in the community. He testified that he had never seen the plaintiff or agreed to pay for the fertilizer, which the tenant had purchased on his own account. Counsel for the defendant, in his argument to the jury, after extolling the high character of his minister client, declared that he had told the truth about the matter, and looking at the plaintiff, who had only one eye, said, "Gentlemen of the Jury, from the evidence in this case, you should not believe a word that this horse-trading, one-eyed son-of-a-bitch has told you." Whereupon plaintiff's counsel appealed to the Court for protection.

The judge, who had been reading a newspaper, asked counsel what had been said, and when told, he adjusted his spectacles, leaned over the bench, and looking at the plaintiff, said, "Well, he hasn't got but one eye, has he?"

Another story that went the rounds was one told of a new minister who took charge of a mountain church. On his first Sunday service he was preaching to the congregation on how desirable it was that good will and kindly feelings prevail among the members. He said he realized that we created enmities during life and that there was probably no one in the congregation who did not have an enemy. To emphasize his point, he asked that if there was anybody in the congregation who did not have an enemy he would stand up. An old brother in the rear of the church stood up and announced that he had no enemies. The parson called him to the pulpit and said that it was a most remarkable fact and that he wanted him to tell the congregation how he had lived so as not to create any enemies. "Well," said the brother, "I'm eighty years old, and the reason I haven't any enemies is that I have outlived the sons of bitches."

Judge Boyd lived to a ripe old age and was succeeded on the Federal bench by Johnson J. Hayes, a partner of mine. Throughout these years, although Boyd was a Republican and I a Democrat, our friendship continued unabated to the end.

In fact, while I have always been strictly a party man, I have had an affinity for "pet" Republicans, and, as my record discloses, have usually had one of them as a partner. When I began the practice of law as a youngster, I was associated with Colonel Winstead, a prominent Republican who had been collector of internal revenue under Grant. My first partner in Greensboro, Colonel Boyd, was a distinguished Republican, and when he was appointed to the Federal judgeship for Western North Carolina, I selected as his successor a prominent Republican and national committeeman, Johnson J. Hayes of Wilkesboro. He remained with me until Congress created the Middle District of North Carolina and he was appointed United States judge. Finally I chose Kenneth M. Brim, a practicing lawyer in Greensboro and referee in bankruptcy under Judge Hayes. This mixture of political affiliations was mentally stimulating and provided a broader approach in the problems of the firm. Incidentally it proved to be good business.

7

Story of a Piedmont Town

GUILFORD COUNTY was formed in 1770. Its county seat was then established as a small settlement centered around Guilford Court House, later named Martinsville in honor of Governor Alexander Martin. In 1808 the General Assembly authorized the moving of the county seat to the center of the county, and the new town was named Greensboro after General Nathanael Greene, hero of the famous Revolutionary Battle of Guilford Court House. Although this battle was inconclusive, it so weakened and retarded the British army under Lord Cornwallis that it proved to be the last important battle of the Revolution, hastening the surrender of Cornwallis at Yorktown. The scene of the battle is now a national military park, with many statues of Revolutionary soldiers including an imposing equestrian statue of General Greene.

The history of Greensboro is unique. To understand its story one must look back to the early settlers of the county. The territory now comprising Guilford County was formerly a part of Rowan and Orange counties, which included a great expanse of piedmont North Carolina inhabited by Indians and abundantly supplied with wild game. Into this territory about the middle of the eighteenth century, came groups of settlers from Pennsylvania—Scotch-Irish Presbyterians, German Lutherans, and Quakers. The Presbyterians settled on Buffalo and Alamance creeks, not far from what is now Greensboro. The German settlement was to the east of Greensboro, and the Quaker settlement to the west.

These early settlers dared to brave the wilderness, with all its dangers and hardships, in order to build a community dedicated to liberty and religious freedom. They everlastingly believed in God and education. Religion and education they sternly maintained, and these, from generation to generation, their descendants have honored.

The story of early Guilford County and Greensboro is so inseparably connected with the life and labors of David Caldwell that special mention of this remarkable man is imperative. David Caldwell was born on a farm in Lancaster County, Pennsylvania, in 1725. He attended the College of New Jersey, now Princeton University, where in 1761 he was graduated. After graduation he tutored at the college while studying for the ministry.

A colony from Pennsylvania had earlier come to North Carolina and had purchased a boundary of land on North Buffalo and Reedy Fork creeks in what is now Guilford County. Their settlements were known as Buffalo and Alamance. In 1765 they invited Caldwell to become their minister. He accepted and settled about three miles west of the present Greensboro. In 1767 he established one of the first classical schools in North Carolina, and conducted it in a log cabin. Young men from all over the South attended the school, and from it went five governors of different states. Others became

United States senators, congressmen, judges, and lawyers. Historians assert that Caldwell's "log college" was the most famous school south of the Potomac. It served as an academy, a college, and a theological seminary, and was the recruiting station for practically all the leading Presbyterian ministers of his day, not only in North Carolina but throughout the South.

There were few doctors in the colony; so Caldwell studied medicine and practiced it far and near. By the time of the Revolution he had acquired a fine library and had enlarged his school. He was an ardent Revolutionist and attended as a delegate the Halifax Convention, which wrote our first constitution. When the British invaded this section, Cornwallis offered a reward for Caldwell's capture, and the soldiers burned his library and forced him to flee for his life. It is said that after the Battle of Guilford Court House he attended the wounded, and, together with the British officers, cut off legs and arms, which were hauled away in wagons. His influence as educator, divine, and physician has left an indelible impression upon Guilford County and Greensboro.

In 1810, the University of North Carolina made him an honorary Doctor of Divinity and he was considered for the presidency of that institution. He went to bed at ten o'clock, and arose at four, to begin work. He lived to be ninety-nine years old. Commentators have freely asserted that considering his long life of active service, and the schools in which he taught the classics and divinity so long, he was probably one of the greatest men North Carolina has had.

An interesting story is told of an occurrence at the Guilford Court House before its removal to Greensboro. Judge Spruce Macay (pronounced McCoy) was holding court, and wished to appoint a permanent clerk of the court. There were several candidates, but he finally sent for Dr. Caldwell, who had been his former teacher, and asked if one of his sons would not make a suitable clerk for the office. The Doctor thought not, as none of them had had any special training for such a job. The Judge insisted that he think it over and report to him the next day. Dr. Caldwell returned the next morning with his son Thomas, saluted the Judge, and said, "Well, Judge, here he is—I have done the best I could." The Judge appointed Thomas Caldwell, and he held the office for forty years.

One of Thomas Caldwell's first duties was to record the admission of Andrew Jackson to practice law before the court. He inscribed in the court records the following entry: "Andrew Jackson produced a license from the Judges of the Superior Court of law and equity to practice law, and was admitted as an attorney of this court, November 21, 1787."

Dr. Caldwell was minister of the two churches, Buffalo and Alamance, for over half a century. The Presbyterians built the first church in Greensboro. It was organized by six women, two men, and four Negro slaves. They naturally named it the First Presbyterian Church. It has grown and prospered until this day. As the population grew, other denominations built churches until it is believed that there are more churches in Greensboro today than in any other town in the state. The religious influence of the early settlers is still manifest in the regularity and number of church attendance.

In the early part of the nineteenth century, another notable character came along—a Quaker and a man of ability and force. His name was Dr. Nereus Mendenhall. He was active among the Quakers and in 1837 helped found the New Garden School, which in time became Guilford College, an institution which has always exerted a wholesome influence in Greensboro and the state.

The impetus given by Dr. Caldwell to the educational life of Guilford County and the South continued into the 1800's. To carry on the work that he had so long conducted, the Greensboro Academy was chartered in 1816. The Reverend William D. Paisley, in 1820, organized a school for boys. In 1833 the Orange Presbytery resolved to build a classical school for males. It was named for Dr. Caldwell and was known as the Caldwell Institute. In 1820 Thomas Caldwell, a son of David, donated the site for a school for girls, which was opened and successfully operated until John M. Morehead, who had just been elected governor of the state, erected, in 1840, a four-story brick building on West Market Street and established Edgeworth Female Seminary to succeed it. In 1850 Professor Richard Sterling took over the school and operated it until 1862, when the war closed most of the schools in the South. In 1843 the cornerstone was laid for Greensboro Female College, which is still an outstanding Methodist school for girls. It was the first college for women in the state to confer the A.B. degree. Greensboro, through the years a leader in education, gave to the state in 1852 its first superintendent of common schools, Calvin H. Wiley, of Guilford College.

The Civil War suspended most of the South's internal activities, but in 1870 Greensboro opened her system of graded schools for both races, giving the colored children their *pro rata* share of the school funds. In 1875 a vote was held to ratify an amendment increasing the tax rate on real estate 25¢ per $100 for both races, and only eight votes were cast against it. In 1891 this city voted a bond issue of $30,000 to secure the State Normal and Industrial College, and not a single vote was cast against it. This college, now a part of the University of North Carolina, was built and its destiny shaped by the great Dr. Charles D. McIver. The selecting of Greensboro as the site for this school proved a happy choice, and the school itself became a powerful force in the great educational renaissance in North Carolina.

McIver, by his indomitable will, broke the shackles of prejudice and gave to the women of the state a new hope and to Greensboro the leadership in the education of women. The College now has an enrollment of over three thousand girls—one of the largest colleges for women in the South.

In 1891 only one vote was recorded against a similar donation to the state Agricultural and Technical College for the colored race. In 1889 the state chartered Bennett College, engaged in Christian education of the colored race. It has grown to take its place among the principal schools of the country for the education of Negro women.

The significance of all this is that it shows Greensboro's devotion to education and, what is more important, its purpose to educate the Negroes as well as the whites. This has been her answer to the so-called Negro problem. From the organization of the First Presbyterian Church, with four of its twelve members Negro slaves, down to the present, Greensboro has had no Negro problem. The rights of the Negroes are respected; they are encouraged in all of their worthy undertakings; and be it said to their everlasting credit, Greensboro has had no race riots or unseemly complications between the races. They pay no poll tax and vote in all of our elections.

The names of the men who shaped the destinies of Guilford County and Greensboro for one hundred years form a roster of which any community should feel proud. Let me list a few of the most conspicuous. In the early days there were David Caldwell, Nereus Mendenhall, and Nathan Hunt, and later among the dominies were William D. Paisley, John A. Gretter, Eli Carruthers, and Jacob Henry Smith.

Greensboro, up to 1855, was without railroads. Governor John M. Morehead was the father of the North Carolina Railroad running from Goldsboro through Greensboro to Charlotte. Later, during the Civil War, a military road was built from Danville to Greensboro, and still later the Cape Fear & Yadkin Valley was built connecting Mount Airy with Greensboro and Wilmington in the hope of supplying transportation from the granaries of the Middle West to the seacoast. The chief actors in this enterprise in Greensboro were Julius A. Gray, Dr. W. A. Lash, Dr. Evan Benbow, and their associates.

The bar of Greensboro has been noted for its ability and learning. The two most conspicuous members of this bar prior to the Civil War were John A. Gilmer and John M. Morehead. Gilmer had been a member of Congress and was personally known to President Lincoln. Lincoln offered him a seat in his cabinet, which Gilmer declined, but his name and fame stand at the top. Governor Morehead, with his ability as a barrister and his sound judgment in statecraft, employed both to the renown of his state. The extension of the railroad from Goldsboro to the east resulted in its terminal's being named for him—Morehead City.

Before 1900 Greensboro supplied four members of the State Supreme Court—Judges Robert P. Dick, John H. Dillard, Thomas Settle, and Robert M. Douglas. Judge Douglas was a son of Stephen A. Douglas, the Little Giant, who, while a member of Congress, married Miss Martha Martin of Rockingham County, North Carolina. Judge Douglas was a private secretary to President Grant for eight years, and after his father's death he made Greensboro his home and married a daughter of Judge Dick. Two of his sons are still living in Greensboro—Martin and Robert D. Douglas—and are members of the local bar. Robert was for a while attorney general of the state. Judge

Dick was named Federal judge for Western North Carolina when that district was formed in 1872.

Along with these were other lawyers who attained eminence at the bar; chief among them were Colonel James T. Morehead; Judge David Schenck, Colonel Boyd, Colonel Staples, Colonel John A. Barringer, and, a little later, Judge Bynum and others. Judges Dick and Dillard established a law school—the leading institution of its kind in the state—which they conducted for a number of years.

About 1890 Greensboro began to attract men and capital in in the business world. Its population increased rapidly and its factories steadily multiplied. The Cones were the leaders in the industrial awakening. They built what is now the largest denim business in the world. Moses Cone was the leading genius in this undertaking and, with his brothers, put Greensboro on the industrial map. When he died, he left an estate now estimated at $16,000,000 for the erection and maintenance of the Cone Hospital, to perpetuate his memory.

Among the local business enterprises in the early 1880's, there was one destined to become famous—the Porter Drug Store. This was the rallying point for the doctors, lawyers, and town gossips, who gathered there in the afternoon and swapped "lies." Employed in the drugstone was a youth named William Sydney Porter, an embryo artist who drew sketches of first one and then another, and particularly of those calling for a doctor. He became quite a local character before he moved to Texas. After many vicissitudes he ended as one of the great short story writers of the nation. Greensboro, years later, named its first modern hotel for him—the O. Henry.

Greensboro, as I first knew it, had four thousand inhabitants. Now, in the city and its environs, there are a hundred thousand. And among the business enterprises today are four which are particularly noteworthy: the Vick Chemical Company, a nationally known concern; the Cone Export and Commission Company, which manufactures 25 per cent of all the denim made in the United States; Burlington Mills, an internationally known organization with seventy-five plants; and J. F. Stephens Company, a nationally known textile concern.

When I came to Greensboro in May, 1897, I was a struggling young lawyer, unmindful of its past or its future, with everything to gain and nothing to lose.

8

Campaign of 1898—A Lucky Break

THE Fusion combination of Republicans and Populists in 1896 gave the Democratic party the most complete and humiliating defeat any political party has ever taken in the long history of the state. The Fusionists captured all the state offices from governor down, a big majority of both branches of the General Assembly, every congressman except Kitchin, nearly all the county offices, and both United States senators.

As the campaign of 1898 approached, the Democrats were depressed and disheartened. The political future, as a cynic expressed it, "looked as dark as midnight and as black as hell." In the midst of this gloom, the old war horses of the party, fearing defeat, shunned a nomination for even the most attractive offices. In these circumstances, the ninth judicial district, of which Greensboro was a member, nominated Thomas J. Shaw, a political novice, for judge, and R. B. Boone, an erratic criminal lawyer from Durham, for solicitor.

When the campaign opened, Boone attended a political rally in Chatham County and in an intemperate speech assailed the

Populists for fusing with the Republicans. The crowd was strongly Populist; they denounced him, and in disgust he resigned the nomination. Under the party organization the judicial committee for the district was called to meet in Durham to nominate his successor. Here we had a vacancy for solicitor, the best-paying office in the state, in the largest and richest district in the state, and apparently nobody was willing to take a chance at winning it.

Having nothing to lose, I set about to secure the nomination. Through the influence of friends, the committee nominated me even though it resulted in selecting both the judge and the solicitor of the district from the same county.

There soon followed a complete state organization of the Democrats, with F. M. Simmons, who later became United States senator, at its head. He was a master organizer and political strategist, and, after drawing around him as consultants the shrewdest men in the party, decided to make a frontal and daring attack against Governor Daniel L. Russell and his administration. The Governor had become very unpopular with the masses on account of his appointments of unfit men to office, particularly ignorant Negroes. A scandal in the management of the State Penitentiary broke out, and even the Governor was quoted as saying "The damned rascals are about to steal the Pen." Another of his complaints was that in many of the counties in the eastern part of the state there were not enough decent Republicans to fill the offices.

The legislature had changed the election laws so as to allow illiterate Negroes by the thousands to vote, thus putting the white people, in a number of counties where they were in the minority, under the political domination of the Negroes. Taking advantage of this situation, the Democratic organization, which was beginning to click, struck upon the idea of organizing a white supremacy campaign, with its chief slogan, "This is a white man's country, and by the help of God it shall be a white man's government."

By now many of the Populists were getting sick of fusion with the Republicans, and the unfolding scandals drove many of the better elements of the party back to their first love—the Democrats.

But the deciding factor, which was to terminate in a political revolution and sweep the Fusionists from power, was what came to be known as the red shirt campaign. All through the eastern part of the state, in the so-called black belt, Democrats organized, dressed themselves out in red shirts, and toured the country making inflammatory speeches denouncing the Fusion regime, depicting the scandals and horrors which flowed from putting into public office ignorant Negroes and sorry white men associated with them. In some sections there was violence and bloodshed, which resulted in many Negroes' staying away from the polls on election day. In Wilmington, the home of Governor Russell, bitterness and disorder took on its most savage form and a few deaths were later reported. A famous leader of the red shirts in that section was afterwards taunted with the charge that in Wilmington they shot Negro voters with cannon. "No," replied he. "All we did was on election morning fire a volley of cannon simply to assure the Negroes that we were going to have a fair election that day."

Behind all this, however, were two mighty forces supporting the campaign, forces that the public did not know of until years afterwards, and of which I, a newcomer and tenderfoot, was blissfully ignorant. It was deep-sea stuff, which, coming to light many years later, had still lost none of its odor.

One of these forces was the large financial contribution to the campaign by railroads in the state in consideration of a promise by Simmons, the state chairman, that if he were elected, the General Assembly would not disturb the low tax rates against their property. Colonel A. B. Andrews of Raleigh, vice president of the Southern Railroad, was the spokesman for all the railroads and had a close tie-in with the American Tobacco Company through the Dukes, who, though Republicans, like Andrews never allowed political principles to interfere with making or saving money.

The other force was an alliance between Simmons and Dr. John C. Kilgo and Josiah W. Bailey. Dr. Kilgo was president of Trinity College, a Methodist institution, and himself a famous evangelist. Josiah W. Bailey was editor of the *Biblical Recorder,* the Baptist organ of the state. These two worthies became the leaders of their respective denominations in the state in a bitter fight against state aid to higher education in North Carolina, which involved at that time the very existence of the University in Chapel Hill and the institutions now known as the Woman's College in Greensboro, and State College in Raleigh. Simmons realized the value to his party's cause of the two great denominations, and in order to get their support he entered into a deal with Kilgo and Bailey that if they would back his campaign he would agree beforehand that the General Assembly to be elected would not make any additional appropriations to the cause of higher education in the state. Kilgo, Bailey, and Andrews were all gold bugs, as was Simmons, and, as Theodore Roosevelt said to E. H. Harriman, they were "practical men." Simmons operated on the principle that the end justifies the means, whatever the price. The end was a complete victory. On the morning following the election I awoke to find myself elected for four years solicitor of the ninth judicial district, comprising eight large counties in the richest and most populous section of the state.

9

Schooling of a Prosecuting Attorney

For an inexperienced youngster of twenty-seven the office of solicitor was a severe challenge and a heavy responsibility. The criminal dockets of my courts embraced all offenses arising in the district from carrying concealed weapons to rape and murder. My predecessors had always been able and experienced lawyers, and the bar of the district, with which I was to measure swords, was recognized as the ablest in the state, and in those days its members appeared regularly as counsel in criminal cases. I resolved to give the job all that was in me, which often—to my chagrin—I found was for a while not enough. A few of the cold-blooded brothers of the bar frequently made me live hard, taking advantage of my inaptness and slurring at my mistakes. But as time wore on and familiarity with the duties and procedure of my office increased, I began to grow spurs which ultimately proved useful.

My first great legal battle standing toe-to-toe took place in Durham in the trial of the famous case of *State* v. *Murray*. The defendant was a prosperous and influential merchant charged with murdering his uncle, an equally prominent citizen and his competitor in business, by shooting him to death in an altercation on the streets of the city. Local excitement and feeling ran high, and the defendant engaged every experienced lawyer at the bar (twelve in number) to defend him. The sympathy of the public was so strongly with the defendant that even the officers of the court hesitated to render me the customary assistance in preparation of the case for trial. Many prominent citizens urged me not to prosecute the case, but a careful study of the evidence satisfied me that Murray was guilty at least of manslaughter.

The trial lasted eight days, and it was a bitter contest, in which no quarter was asked and no favors given. Among the lawyers for the defense were a number of the ablest in the state, ex-Judge R. W. Winston, V. S. Bryant, Major W. B. Guthrie, R. B. Boone, J. S. Manning, and the Fuller brothers. I realized that it was to be the severest test of my young life, and that, in the language of Daniel Webster in a statement to an associate on the eve of his famous reply to Hayne, "Some buck must die this day." I developed the State's case and the learned presiding Judge Peebles held that it was sufficient to take the case to the jury. The defendant had many witnesses of unimpeachable character who began giving their version of the shooting, tending to show that the killing was accidental, resulting from a scuffle between the defendant and the deceased over the possession of the pistol.

After adjournment of court one day, a witness for the defendant innocently remarked in my hearing that Judge Winston had the night before called all the witnesses for the defense to his office and that they had a rehearsal of the scene of the homicide and the part that each witness would testify to.

This gave me a clue to work on, and when Judge Winston

the next day turned over to me his witness for cross-examination, I began by asking him if he was one of the actors in the rehearsal in Judge Winston's office. The result was electrical. Winston and two or three of his associates all objected at once to the question, and the atmosphere was lurid with denunciation of my insinuation. The question was declared highly improper; it was said to impugn the character of the witness and the conduct of counsel.

I replied that no reflections were intended, but that such proceedings were something new in North Carolina and that the jury was entitled to know what part each witness played in this drama under Judge Winston's direction and what each one said, in order to compare these statements with the testimony of other witnesses. Judge Peebles held the question competent and directed me to proceed. The jury became terribly interested in each witness's recital of what occurred in the lawyer's office, which was sometimes amusing and sometimes ridiculous. The effect was devastating to the seriousness of the defense.

The debate of counsel to the jury centered around the question as to who actually had control of the pistol when the fatal shot was fired. The defendant's counsel contended that the evidence showed that the deceased drew the pistol and the defendant grabbed it to prevent being shot, and that while the pistol was still in deceased's hand it was accidentally discharged, killing him. The solicitor for the State contended that the defendant, who was a powerful man physically and much younger than his uncle, had actually disarmed the deceased and had possession of the pistol when the fatal shot was intentionally fired.

My demonstration of the State's contentions before the jury resulted in an unusual incident. The jury panel was seated immediately in front of the speaker on the same floor level, and the area was carpeted by a heavily corded rug. Holding in my hand the .44 bulldog pistol in evidence, I reminded the jury that all the witnesses agreed that when the fatal shot was fired the deceased threw up both hands crying out, "My God I am killed!" and fell to the pavement; that if the pistol at that moment had been in the hands of the deceased when he threw up his hands, this is what would have occurred: Raising both hands above my head with the pistol in the right hand, I let it fall, as if from the deceased's hand, to the floor immediately in front of the jurors. When it struck the corded rug it bounced three feet in the air and bounced again and again before it settled at the jurors' feet. The clerk of the court, observing the scene (I later learned), remarked to the Sheriff, "That finishes this case for the defendant."

The jury convicted Murray of manslaughter. I shall never forget the remark of one of the opposing counsel, Jones Fuller, the following morning when he came into court looking dispirited. "Good morning, Jones. I hope you feel well this morning," said I. "No," he replied, "I feel like hell, and I want to say that personally I am fond of you, but as solicitor, God damn you."

A story was told of Judge Winston, leading counsel in this case, that Abe Max, a merchant Jew in Durham, employed the Judge to collect a $5,000 policy of fire insurance for damages to his stock of goods. There was a serious question about the origin of the fire, and the insurance company refused to pay. Judge Winston brought suit and recovered the full amount. He notified Max to come to his office for a settlement. When Max arrived, the money was counted out in two piles of $2,500 each. The Judge explained to Max the great difficulty he had in collecting the money and said that he had divided it so that Max would receive $2,500 and he would retain $2,500 as his compensation. Max was horrified and threw up his hands and said, "My God, Judge, who was burned out, you or me?"

Many of the nation's greatest jurists and statesmen attribute much of their success to the schooling they received as young prosecuting attorneys. As spokesman for the State the prosecuting attorney is chief actor from day to day and from year to year in the forum established by law to administer justice, protect society, and punish the wrongdoers. The criminal court is composed of a complete cross-section of the community's life and deeds. In these tribunals we see reviewed and exposed the passions, prejudices, and criminal instincts of men and women —human nature in the raw. Disposing of a thousand cases a year as I did revealed many tragedies and heart-breaks, the indiscretions of youth, the vices of middle age, and the wantonness of old offenders. But sordid as much of it was, still there remains photographed in my memory striking scenes and occurrences which lent humor, mirth, wit, and even philosophy to the court proceedings.

Illustrative was a case tried in Oxford, where a prominent farmer was indicted for committing adultery with his tenant's wife. The State's evidence showed that the defendants had spent the night together in a farmhouse near Oxford. Judge A. W. Graham, a handsome, dignified man, appeared as counsel for the accused. His defense to this specific act was that the defendants had driven a mule and buggy to Oxford and that on their return the mule got sick and they had to spend the night at a farmhouse in which there was only one spare room and bed; that while they occupied the same bed, both defendants, as a manifestation of their prudence and complete innocence, testified that upon retiring the *feme* turned her face to the wall and so remained until morning. In addressing the jury I repeated a little ditty which seemed appropriate to the occasion: "God made Adam in his own image and placed him in the Garden of Eden. He then made Eve and clothed her in fig leaves. When Eve first saw Adam she turned her face to the wall, because she knew something would be doing when the leaves began to fall."

At another term of this court, the solicitor, who is popularly regarded as a hard-hearted and relentless prosecutor, had an opportunity to do a kindly turn in justice to an oppressed Negro share-cropper who was indicted for removing a part of his crop without paying rent. Satisfied that the offense was only technical, the judge upon my recommendation suspended judgment allowing the defendant to go home, harvest his crop, and report to the court that he had made good his contractual obligations to his harsh landlord. After court adjourned, the defendant's wife, who had shown deep concern over their plight, called at my office to thank me for saving her and five children from being turned out of house and home. Noticing that she was big with child I told her to go home, have her baby, obey the judgment of the court, and all would be well. Her face lighted up and as a token of her appreciation she said, "I will have the baby, and if it is a boy I have already selected its name —Judge Solicitor." I afterwards learned that the judge and I had a namesake in that county.

10

Parting of the Ways

WHETHER or not "there is a tide in the affairs of men which taken at the flood leads on to fortune" or a divinity that shapes our ends, it is certainly true that in politics it is fatal to back the wrong horse. The position of solicitor for the ninth judicial district, embracing the counties of Guilford, Alamance, Caswell, Orange, Durham, Chatham, Person, and Granville, gave me a certain political state-wide influence.

In 1900 F. M. Simmons, who had led the Democratic party to a triumphant victory in 1898 over the combined forces of the Republicans and Populists, was a candidate to succeed Marion Butler as United States senator. The other candidate for this high office was General Julian S. Carr of Durham, an ex-Confederate soldier, head of the Bull Durham Tobacco Company, a loyal Democrat, and a personal friend of mine. When I was a youngster, living in Roxboro and struggling to accumulate enough money to defray my college expenses, he had given me an order to buy for his company 100,000 pounds of leaf tobacco on the Roxboro market. Carr had been a liberal contributor to the party chest for many years and was recognized as fit for the office. I felt that I was in honor and gratitude bound to support him.

Never to be forgotten was a fateful visit by Judge T. B. Womack, a Simmons supporter, to see me at Chatham Court, where I was prosecuting the criminal docket. He said that Simmons had asked him to solicit my support of his candidacy; that Simmons on account of his party service in the white supremacy campaign two years before was entitled to be nominated for the Senate; that as chairman of the state Democratic executive committee he had complete control of the party organization; that General Carr, while a fine man, had no organization and could not possibly win. In my youthful innocence and inexperience in the sordid game of machine politics, I totally missed the import of his argument. I frankly explained to Judge Womack my situation; that General Carr was my neighbor and long-time friend; that I appreciated the splendid service Simmons had rendered the party, but that I could not in good conscience turn my back on Carr. Little did I then know that the word conscience is not to be found in any political lexicon and that this decision was to mean a parting of the ways with the most powerful and ruthless political machine that the state has ever known.

For the next thirty years, while Simmons remained in the Senate, he was to be my political foe—he never forgave or forgot. Whether I was a candidate for Congress in 1908 or in a primary fight in 1920 to succeed Lee S. Overman in the United States Senate, the hand of revenge was to be ever raised against me. We lived in different sections of the state and rarely met; our differences were solely political and not personal. As the years passed, evidence accumulated, demonstrating our total incompatibility in thinking, ideals, and philosophy of government. To begin with, Simmons was a stand-pat, hard-boiled conservative; he detested Bryan, disliked Wilson, hated the Populists and all would-be reformers.

For those of us who espoused the liberalism of Jefferson, followed the leadership of Bryan, admired the judicial statesmanship of Walter Clark, and opposed machine-controlled politics, Simmons had little respect and no regard. His machine was perfectly integrated and abundantly financed by the railroads, trusts, liquor interests, and other big business. They never worked at cross purposes or took anything for granted.

Shortly after becoming solicitor, I had an offer of one of these sugar-coated pills in the shape of a free pass on the Southern Railroad lines. The Southern Railroad System extended through the heart of my district and a free pass meant a considerable saving in expense in reaching my courts.

Colonel A. B. Andrews of Raleigh was head of the Southern Railroad and political generalissimo of the Atlantic Coastline and the Seaboard Air Line, as well as the Page Railroad. When I came into office the railroads in North Carolina were issuing, according to the Railroad Commission's finding, a hundred thousand free passes, in violation of law, to editors, lawyers, ministers, and business men of influence. One day I received a letter from F. H. Busbee of Raleigh, assistant division counsel of the Southern, offering me a free pass. I thanked him but declined to accept it.

Some months later, while I was engaged in court at Oxford, Captain Charles Price, chief counsel for the Southern in North Carolina, called on me for a conference. He opened the conversation by saying that he wished to employ me as counsel for his company, which would entitle me to a free pass; that the judges and solicitors in the state rode on free passes, and that he would like to give me one over his railroad. When I questioned the propriety of it, he suggested that they would make me a special assistant counsel, which would take care of that phase of the matter. As I remained silent he raised his ante saying that in addition he would give me and my family free Pullman passes over other railroads when I wished to take trips.

"What, Captain Price," I asked, "am I expected to do in consideration for these great favors?" If I had struck him in the face with a wet towel he would not have looked more abashed.

I thanked him for his generous offer but reminded him that the railroad already had counsel in every county of my district besides several special counsel, and that without regard to what other solicitors did I thought it improper for me to accept so much to do so little and thus place myself as a public servant under obligation to his road, which occasionally appeared on my criminal docket as a defendant. This decision was further motivated by the knowledge that the railroads not only were operating transportation systems but were dominating both the Democratic and Republican parties, controlling conventions and secretly dictating candidates for offices.

The conference ended, but the railroad's opposition to my political ambitions stood from that day. Those were the daring days of the reckless nineties, when high finance and low morals dominated politics, business, and government.

What I didn't then know was that the creed of all political machines is that whosoever is not for you is against you. My deciding not to support Simmons for the Senate and to take a pocketful of free passes from the railroads completed the circuit, and thereafter this aggregation regarded me a political Ishmaelite.

In 1901 my wife, Maude Harris, who had not been in good

health, died, leaving me with our infant son Robert. As I was an only child, my father and mother, who were living in Durham where my father was superintendent of health, removed to Greensboro to make us a permanent home.

11

Plowing New Ground

TRYING important criminal cases day after day, matching arguments and wits with the leaders of the bar, was a fascinating business and so absorbing that few solicitors paid any attention to the tedious and prosaic work of the civil law. Wishing to avoid this mistake, I accepted employment and attended to such civil business as came my way.

In 1901 I instituted a suit for a Mrs. Gorrell against the Greensboro Water Company that went through all the courts, state and Federal, ending in her favor five years later in the Supreme Court of the United States. This case, on account of its novel character and the refined questions of law involved, became a legal landmark in the state under the name of *"Gorrell* v. *Water Co.,"* and is still studied in our law schools. A companion case, *Fisher* v. *Water Co.,* was later brought, and after judgments were obtained against the company in the state court, both cases were transferred to the Federal court and consolidated.

It was my first big law suit, and was brought against the advice of older brethren of the bar, who did not think a valid cause of action existed. The facts were these: Mrs. Gorrell's storehouse and Captain Fisher's hotel, the Guilford, had both been destroyed by fire on account of the failure of the Water Company to furnish a sufficient water supply and pressure even to extinguish the burning awnings. The Water Company was a foreign-owned corporation, operating under a franchise contract with the city. The company took the position that it had no contract with individual property owners and had received no compensation from them; that no privity of contract existed in their favor; that the city alone could sue for its failure to perform; and that the city had suffered enough. A study of the law involved disclosed that no similar case had ever been tried in North Carolina, and that the reported cases from other jurisdictions showed that in instances where like suits had been brought, a recovery had been denied.

But in my search I came upon an opinion by the great Judge Seymour Thompson dealing with this question, in which, while denying recovery, he said that if the suit had been brought against the company for the negligent non-performance of a public duty owed to property owners, and then set up the contract between the Water Company and the city as an inducement to the obligation, a different result might have been reached.

The complaints in both cases were made to rest upon Judge Thompson's dictum in that case, and it served me as a guardian angel through all the courts and against a battery of the most eminent lawyers in the state and from the Baltimore bar. The checkered career of this unusual case constitutes a legal saga in American jurisprudence, twice heard by the Supreme Court of North Carolina, twice by the United States Circuit Court of Appeals in Richmond, and finally by the Supreme Court of the

United States, and in each instance the plaintiffs won by a divided court. Years later the United States Supreme Court, in a somewhat similar case, by a divided court reversed itself.

It was agreed at the outset that my compensation should be a part of the recovery, contingent upon our winning. The clients paid my fee gladly, and the amount received tended to remind me, considering my first year's receipts at the bar—$265—that it was a long way from Roxboro to Greensboro.

A very unusual case occurred in Greensboro while I was solicitor. A Dr. Matthews had previously moved from Pittsboro to Greensboro and had established a good practice. He was a likeable man and had made a number of friends. The town was shocked to hear that his wife had died under mysterious circumstances and that he was under suspicion as the murderer. An investigation promptly followed and these are some of the material circumstances: Dr. Matthews and his wife had both been taking morphine, and on the day of the homicide they were both under its influence. The neighbors had become suspicious and called Dr. Turner and my father, Dr. Brooks, who found the wife unconscious and desperately ill. Dr. Matthews was in his pajamas and scurrying from room to room talking disconnectedly, apparently unconscious of his wife's condition. Dr. Turner was standing by her bed, when Dr. Matthews came and sat down on the bed, saying he wanted to feel his wife's pulse. He slipped his hand under the cover, and Dr. Turner, noticing a quick movement of the cover, grabbed Matthews' hand and threw back the cover. There in the husband's hand was a syringe which he had unloaded into his wife's arm. A few hours later she died, and he was arrested and jailed for murder.

There was naturally much speculation over the case and especially as to whether the syringe with which he administered the last shot contained strychnine or morphine. The difference between the symptoms of poisoning from strychnine or from morphine thus assumed a large place in the trial. During the long trial the courtroom was crowded. W. A. Guthrie from Durham and Charles M. Stedman from the Guilford bar were counsel for the defendant. As the trial progressed I noticed that a number of doctors were in attendance in court and one of them, Dr. Bell, was called as a witness. He testified that the symptoms of poisoning by morphine were substantially the same as those of poisoning by strychnine. Dr. Bell was a prominent physician and the other doctors were waiting to give like testimony. I felt sure that he was mistaken and that night I got a bright young doctor fresh from the University of Pennsylvania, and had him tutor me on the difference in diagnoses and furnish me with the latest book on the subject.

When court opened the next morning the defendant called another doctor and he followed suit in his testimony. On cross-examination I reached for my medical book and took him step by step, demonstrating the vast difference between the two poisonings. When I had finished with him the perspiration was running down his face and he was completely wilted. No other doctor was examined.

The theory of the State was that Dr. Matthews was jealous of his wife and had threatened to kill her. There was a tense moment in the trial when I offered to prove an overt act. The judge called me to the bench and said that he would write down the testimony as it was going to be pretty rough and we might excuse the court stenographer, who was a charming young woman. I suggested that I speak to the stenographer. Whereupon she said, "I have taken this job. I can pull down this sailor hat over my eyes and take it as it comes." The testimony revealed that the husband returned home unexpectedly, and looking through the first floor window he saw his wife with another man, nude, and the bed reflected in the mirror so as to give a double view of their infidelity.

The jury convicted him of second degree murder and the court gave him twenty years in the State Penitentiary. An appeal to the Supreme Court was taken, but before it was heard he committed suicide.

An excited phone call from a rich young friend asked me to join him that night in a drawing room of the train going South for a very important trip. I found him terribly excited and as nervous as a cat.

He opened the subject by handing me a copy of a summons and complaint in a threatened suit, demanding $100,000 damages for the alienation of the affections of a man's wife. An accompanying letter from a lawyer stated that the papers had not been filed in court, but would be unless he made prompt satisfaction. "What on earth is all this shooting about?" I asked. Here is his jitteringly told story.

Some weeks before, he had met, in another city where he was visiting, a very attractive woman and her husband. He had seen much of them at social functions, and the wife had been particularly gracious to him. Her charm and beauty had intrigued him, and she confided to him that her relations with her husband were not happy, that in a few days she was going for a long stay at her mother's home in Tennessee, but that she would love to see him sometime. The circumstances seemed very propitious, and he suggested that if she would let him know when, he would meet her in Atlanta for a visit and a party. The Atlanta meeting took place a week later.

After a party of three days, he escorted her to the train for

Tennessee. To his amazement, at the train he met her husband, accompanied by a policeman. The wife pretended complete ignorance of the trap, but the husband threatened to have him arrested for adultery with his wife at the hotel where they had registered as man and wife. Faced with such an exposé and scandal, my client had sought to pay his way out, and after some horse-trading as to amount, he gave the aggrieved and injured husband his due bill for $6,000, not having that much loose cash on his person. The love-nest thus rudely broken up, his lady-love, still protesting her innocence and regrets, took the train for Tennessee. The compensated and (as he thought) satisfied husband disappeared with the policeman, leaving him disgusted, but wiser and poorer.

All this was water gone under the bridge. What was paralyzing him now was how to avoid a $100,000 damage suit, with its attendant publicity and disgrace to his wife and valued family connections.

His authority to me was to see the lawyer and settle the case out of court, whatever the cost. I told him to calm down, that the very fact of the lawyer's sending him the complaint and demand before actually instituting the suit showed on its face that it was what lawyers call a "strike suit," and that since, as I learned, the man and his wife were living together, they did not want publicity either, but rather were trying to blackmail him on the q.t. out of more money, because they knew he was rich. I advised him, however, that since they had agreed on the balm price of $6,000, even though it was more than value received, he had better pay it. This ended it.

12

The Gold Brick Case

THERE is a quaint old saying among the country people in North Carolina, "There are more ways to kill a dog than by choking him to death on butter." Likewise there are more ways to make money than by selling fake gold brick; yet this project was undertaken in North Carolina in 1902 and resulted in a sensational trial.

The case began before a local justice of the peace in Greensboro, ran the gamut of all the courts, both state and Federal, finally ending after two years in the Supreme Court of the United States.

J. F. Jordan, the sheriff of Guilford County, rushed into my office one afternoon saying that he had just received a phone message from Paul Garrett of Goldsboro to the effect that a professional swindler from the West, representing himself as a miner, was there trying to sell him a gold brick now in the possession of an Indian, who was said to be in hiding on Buffalo Creek near Greensboro; that he and the miner, who was acting as contact man, would arrive in Greensboro on the noon train next day; and that in order to identify himself he would pull a handkerchief from his pocket as he alighted from the train so that the sheriff could follow them to the meeting place with the Indian. We agreed upon the strategy, and Sheriff Jordan selected to accompany him three trusted deputies.

Paul Garrett was a wine manufacturer (who afterwards became a national figure in this business), venturesome, daring, and fearless, as the succeeding events disclosed. Jordan, the sheriff, had the reputation of being the best shot in the county and not afraid of the devil. Armed to the teeth, but dressed in plain clothes, the officers met the train, spotted Garrett and the miner, who were met by a third party with a hack in waiting and were driven away toward Buffalo Creek. The sheriff and his posse in separate buggies, previously arranged for, followed at a distance but always in sight.

When the destination was reached, the miner took Garrett down the creek through a forest and thick underbrush to where the Indian, called Gomez Bona, awaited them. The posse, by a flank movement, secretly followed and waited until the Indian displayed his brick of gold, and, jabbering, began boring for a specimen. Then the officers confronted them with pistols drawn. The Indian and the miner both drew their guns, but seeing that they were covered and outnumbered, submitted to arrest. Garrett then told the sheriff that the scheme was for him to take the boring to an authorized assayer who was then in Greensboro, and if it turned out to be pure gold as represented, he could buy it from the Indian for $8,000, as the Indian was too shy to go to any town and was afraid his possession of so much gold would arouse suspicion and get him into trouble.

The sheriff immediately hurried back to locate the assayer before the arrest became public. He found that a suspicious-looking character had been loitering around the hotel of the town and was then in his room. The assayer was registered under the name of Howard, and when the sheriff went to his room to make the arrest, Howard made for the toilet and undertook to destroy some papers in his possession, the most important one being a forged letter from the Secretary of the United States Treasury vouching for him as a duly appointed assayer for the government. In his baggage was a complete set of equipment for assaying gold, with a package of small gold nuggets. The trick, if it had worked, was to substitute these particles of pure gold for the spurious borings, assay them, and thus demonstrate the genuineness of the gold brick.

Imagine the excitement in a town of twelve thousand when the arrest and the facts became known. It soon developed from telegrams sent by the accused men from jail to Chicago that they had influential connections there who would finance their defense.

The preliminary hearing was held in the county courtroom, and it was packed to the windows with an excited public. Squire Wolfe presided, and the defendants were represented by three of the ablest men at bar. The State's case was presented by me as solicitor, while defendants offered no evidence. The Justice announced that he would hold the defendants for trial in the Superior Court and fix the appearance bond of each at $250.

An amusing incident then occurred. As the crowd hissed its disapproval, the Justice said, "Hold on a minute—I just threw that out as a feeler." He got the "feel," and turning to me said, "Mr. Solicitor, how much do you think the bonds should be?" I replied that the offense was a bold and daring conspiracy to rob a citizen of $8,000 and that the bonds should be large enough to insure their appearance to answer the final judgment of the court. He fixed their bonds at $2,500 each, in default of which they remained in jail. Carter H. Harrison, the mayor of

Chicago, wrote the solicitor that these men lived in Chicago and bore good reputations, and he urged that the amount of their bonds be reduced. At the trial of the case, Carter, a noted Chicago criminal lawyer, appeared with the staff of local counsel.

For three days a legal battle raged, the defense being that the indictment charged a conspiracy to cheat and defraud, which was never consummated; that in North Carolina, to cheat and defraud was only a misdemeanor, while a conspiracy was a felony; that the State could not make a felony out of an offense, which, if completed, was at most a misdemeanor, by charging a conspiracy which was never carried out.

The jury convicted them, and the court sentenced Hawley, the miner, and Gomez Bona, the Indian, to a term of ten years each in the State Penitentiary, and Howard the assayer to a seven-year term.

The case was appealed to the Supreme Court of the state where, in an exhaustive opinion, the conviction was affirmed, designating this case in the reports as "The Gold Brick Case." From there the case was taken to the Federal District Court, and finally to the Supreme Court of the United States, which affirmed the conviction.

As a sequel, none of the three served his full term. The assayer, Howard, after serving two years, died; a year later the Indian, the weakest of the trio, was pardoned; and the miner, on account of a broken leg, was granted a pardon after serving five years.

13

Pass-Toters' Victory

WHEN the Democratic state primary to select a candidate for governor opened in 1904, my neighbor and friend, Major Charles M. Stedman, decided to enter the contest and asked me to manage his state campaign. Major Stedman had a fine record as a Confederate officer, had served a term as lieutenant-governor of the state, and in 1888 had come near the nomination for governor over Daniel G. Fowle. He was strikingly handsome, with courtly manners and a pleasing speaking voice.

The other candidate, R. B. Glenn, was a rough and ready stump speaker, a great prohibitionist, long on jokes and quoting the Bible. But his greatest asset, which the Stedman camp was later to learn to its sorrow, was that as division counsel of the Southern Railway and intimate friend of Colonel Andrews he had an unbeatable force of free-pass-toters—if they decided to put him in.

Stedman's candidacy was at first received with great favor by the public, and was endorsed by most counties as their conventions were held. Our candidate seemed headed for the governor's chair until the political machine began to click. The strategy employed was both bold and brazen.

Colonel Andrews came to Greensboro one night in his private car and sent for Colonel W. H. Osborne, an old friend and political pal of his, who was assisting us in the campaign, and told him his terms. Osborne took the matter up with Stedman, who at once called me into the conference. "Tell Major Stedman," Andrews was reported as saying, "that I am disposed to be friendly to his candidacy and wish to contribute a substantial sum of money to his campaign. I know he has little money and I wish to be certain of his friendship if he is elected governor."

Stedman resented the imputation involved and asked what I thought should be done. I reminded him that his campaign was progressing satisfactorily, that we were winning delegates everywhere, and that if Colonel Andrews and his railroad would keep hands off, he would win the nomination without the use of more money than his personal friends were contributing and without his becoming obligated to the railroads. But if he decided to accept his contribution, I said that I would quietly retire as manager of his campaign, as I could not be a party to it, and let Colonel Osborne, who thought highly of the idea, take over.

"No," said Stedman, "I'll be damned if I do it." He instructed Osborne to tell Colonel Andrews that he didn't need the money and if elected governor he would be fair and just in dealing with the railroads. When Osborne reported this conversation, Andrews replied, "Very well, but I never trust any man in politics who will not accept my money to help him get elected."

The sequel was that Andrews went on to Winston-Salem, the home of Glenn, where a glorified organization was promptly effected and put in motion all over the state, reflecting the free use of money and passes.

As a desperate move to save the situation, Stedman asked me to see Colonel Andrews and assure him that he was not unfriendly to the railroads and if he were elected Andrews need fear no animosity from him. By appointment I called at Andrews' home in Raleigh one night and had a never-to-be-forgotten interview with the great industrial and political mogul. He was most gracious and treated me with delicate consideration, whiskey, and Havana cigars. The conversation ran smoothly until I brought up the Stedman campaign. I delivered Stedman's message and assured him that I knew, as manager of the campaign, that no improper committals of any kind had been made to anyone; that Stedman, like himself, had served in the Confederate Army, was a kindly man, and had no enemies to punish.

"I like Stedman," Andrews replied, "and I regard him as capable." Then he renewed the suggestion, made to Osborne, that he wanted to contribute to Stedman's campaign, and that Stedman's refusal to accept it created a suspicion in his mind. Looking me straight in the eye, with a sardonic smile, he patronizingly said, "Mr. Brooks, after long years of experience, I have found that it is never safe in politics to count a candidate for office your friend to be trusted unless he accepts your money to help him get elected." I respectfully declined his offer.

The convention was held in Greensboro, and to reach it most of the delegates had to travel long distances by rail. Agents of the railroads throughout the state gave a free pass to every delegate who would agree to support Glenn for governor. A joy-ride followed, and when the convention met, the pass-toters had complete charge. Victor Bryant, who put Stedman in nomination, nearly caused a riot when, in closing his speech, he said,

"I nominate Major Charles Manley Stedman, on behalf of those delegates who paid their own way to this convention and did not come on a free pass."

Major Stedman lost the nomination for governor but saved his integrity, and virtue had its reward. Six years later he was nominated and elected to Congress, and remained there until his death.

14

Happenings at Court

THE ten years spent as solicitor were the richest—and in many ways the happiest—of my professional life. The training I received in the constant trial of cases in the courtroom and the intimate association with numerous learned judges and many able lawyers were largely responsible for whatever success I have had at the bar. Among the notable judges that spent six months or more with me were George H. Brown, William A. Hoke, W. R. Allen, R. B. Peebles, Fred Moore, G. S. Ferguson, and B. F. Long.

Those were the horse-and-buggy days when the chief rewards for the lawyer came from his practice in the courtroom. His reputation was measured largely by his ability to examine and cross-examine witnesses and make forensic arguments to the jury. It was a challenging forum, which attracted the ablest men in the profession, and they followed the sittings of the court in surrounding counties much as the Methodist circuit rider attended his churches. The country-town hotel, with its long piazza, was the gathering point between sessions of court, where the judge, the solicitor, and local and visiting attorneys met for social intercourse, repeating experiences, telling jokes, and settling the affairs of state, often continuing beyond midnight. Unfortunately no such scene is now to be found in the South.

Often at these sessions many racy and amusing stories were told of the happenings in court which were indigenous to the particular county in which the incident occurred. The scene of a startling story was Alamance County, where the great Ruffin was attached and fined for contempt of court. While Ruffin was defending the character of a country girl in a sensational trial, her foster father appeared as a witness against her. When Ruffin took him for cross-examination he said to the witness, "I understand that you are this girl's foster father; that she lives in your home, and on the occasion spoken of you saw this young man take her behind the haystack and have intercourse with her, and that you made no effort to protect her and did not protest." When the witness replied, "Yes," to this statement, Ruffin arose from his chair, his face livid with rage and contempt, pointed his long index finger at the witness and shouted, "You damn son of a bitch, leave that witness chair and get out of this courtroom." The Judge fined Ruffin $100 for contempt of court, but he won his case.

An amusing incident arose out of the investigation of a tragedy which had occurred in Caswell County Court. The noted carpetbagger, Judge Albion W. Tourgée, elected during Reconstruction days, was holding court at Yanceyville, when it was called to his attention that a Negro had been recently lynched in the county, in broad daylight on a public highway, for burning a stock barn of his landlord, and that the affair was witnessed by a crowd of over two hundred citizens.

Tourgée summoned the grand jury, called the matter officially to their attention, denounced it as a brutal violation of law, and instructed them that it was their sworn duty to investigate the lynching and return indictments against every man who aided or abetted in it. He also told them to call on the state's solicitor for legal advice on procedure.

Some hours later the grand jury sent for the solicitor, and the foreman asked him if, under the law, it was the duty of a juror to vote to indict himself. "No," replied the solicitor. "A juror is not required to present or indict either himself or his wife." Whereupon, an old fellow sitting cross-legged in the rear of the room uncrossed his legs, shifted a cud of tobacco from one side of his mouth to the other, and complacently said, "Mr. Foreman, if that is so, I will be damned if that don't let a majority of this grand jury out of that lynching."

Colonel John A. Barringer and Judge Spencer B. Adams, both experienced and aggressive criminal lawyers, were appearing on opposite sides in a hotly contested case in Greensboro before Squire Wolfe, a trial magistrate, when this ridiculous occurrence took place:

The lie was passed between the lawyers. Each jumped from his seat, grabbed a chair, and swung at the other. His Honor, Squire Wolfe, was sitting in the bar of the courtroom immediately underneath a suspended glass chandelier. As the swinging chairs simultaneously hit the chandelier a great crash followed, the glass falling all over the Squire. To escape, he vaulted over the railing of the judge's bench, threw up his hands, and excitedly exclaimed, "My God, gentlemen, this must stop—it is unconstitutional!"

A prime story among the lawyers is one told of Judge Bynum. As was Bynum's habit, after office hours he would get out his bottle and with a friend or two proceed to get comfortably mellowed. After one of these parties he called a hack and started home. On his way he noticed a Holiness meeting in progress under a tent. He decided to stop by and see what was going on. He went in and took a seat just as the conductor of the meeting was taking up a collection. The exhorter called on the congregation to make gifts to the Lord and asked how much they would give. Bynum arose and said he would give $25. "God bless you, my brother," said the collector, and came down to get the money. "No," said Bynum, "that was not your proposition. You asked for a contribution to be made to the Lord, and since I expect to see him before you do, I will hand the money to him."

A young lawyer from eastern Carolina came to the Greensboro bar, but after a few years he decided to go back to eastern Carolina and engage in some other business. Judge Bynum had been kind to him and so he told the Judge of his plans and stated that he wanted to turn over his practice to him. This occurred on an occasion when Bynum and his bottle were on most intimate terms. Bynum drew up his stately figure and said, "I deeply appreciate your generosity, but there are a number of other lawyers in town and I must continue to live and practice with them. I suggest that you announce the day of your departure and bring your practice over and turn the damn thing loose on the court green so as to give each lawyer an equal chance at it."

15

A Political Misadventure

FOLLOWING my election in 1898 as solicitor, I was renominated in 1902 and 1906 and elected each time by increased majorities. The office of solicitor was regarded as quasi-judicial and not political; consequently, never having had to fight for it, my education in political manipulation was very deficient.

All of the counties in my judicial district were embraced in the fifth congressional district, represented by W. W. Kitchin. His spectacular victory over Thomas Settle in 1896 had given him a state-wide reputation, which had been increased by his distinguished service in Congress as a liberal. He was an avowed critic of trusts and monopolies, then in their heyday, and particularly of the American Tobacco Company, which was crushing out weakened competitors and piling up untold millions at the expense of North Carolina tobacco farmers by taking their products, in the absence of competition, at starvation prices.

In the meantime, the third congressional district sent Claude Kitchin, a brother of Will, to Congress, where he soon became a leader of the liberals. Later he rose to the chairmanship of the powerful House Ways and Means Committee, a position in which he won, during the Wilson administration, a national reputation.

The Kitchin brothers and Senator Simmons were never political bedfellows, but the machine could not defeat Will or Claude Kitchin for renomination. As the general election of 1908 approached, Will Kitchin, in response to a wide public demand, announced his candidacy for governor. The machine's candidate was Locke Craig, of Asheville, and this precipitated one of the bitterest inter-party contests ever witnessed in the state. Over the advice of some of my older and wiser friends, who regarded the solicitorship as preferable, I announced my candidacy to succeed Kitchin in Congress.

Soon four other candidates announced for the office—General Royster of Oxford, Reuben D. Reid of Rockingham, Cameron Buxton of Winston-Salem, and Professor J. Allen Holt of my home county of Guilford. At the outset I made the fatal mistake of resigning the solicitorship, which emboldened the enemies I had accumulated over the past ten years in the prosecution of the criminal docket, to oppose me openly. I did not then know that the technique of the successful politician is never to resign a good office until he gets his clutches on a better one. My repeated election as solicitor had lulled me into the complacent belief that I could win hands down. I failed to realize the fundamental differences in the offices—one a judicial and the other purely political, which touched the economic and political life of so many people.

The district convention was held in Greensboro, and I was nominated on the first ballot over my four opponents. It settled the nomination, but the decisive victory so irritated my opponents, all of whom were much older than I, that not one of them lifted a hand to help secure my election.

But my troubles had just begun. The Republicans nominated to oppose me John Motley Morehead of Rockingham County (1866-1923), a wealthy textile manufacturer, scion of a prominent North Carolina family, who was backed by the Simmons machine. I was to get my first lesson in the retribution of history. Had I not declined to support Simmons for the Senate in his contest with Carr? Had I not spurned the Railroad's effort to take me into its camp by employing me as special counsel and filling my pockets with free passes? Had I not joined up with the Kitchins as a liberal, and whooped it up for Bryan? Had I not given deadly offense to Colonel Andrews and his railroad by declining to take its money as manager of Stedman's campaign? Had I not spoken all over the district condemning the American Tobacco Trust, which originated with the Dukes of Durham? As the old saying goes, "Chickens always come home to roost," and in coming this time they lit on me.

Secretly organizing without my knowledge and backed with money and free passes, they corralled in support of their "business-man candidate" the anti-Bryan Democrats among the many manufacturers, bankers, and other big business men in the district. Next came the malefactors who had felt the halter of the law draw while I was solicitor. The old-line Republicans meekly followed their lead, keeping in the background so as to create the impression that it was really a contest between two Democrats.

To direct this motley aggregation, they chose a master schemer, W. H. Osborne, ex-mayor of Greensboro and proprietor of Keeley Institute, of which he was an alumnus. Osborne had induced Professor Holt of Guilford County to enter the primary contest against me, had managed his campaign, and was in honor bound to abide by the result of the convention, but a small thing like that never bothered him. Before coming to

Greensboro he had lived in Durham, was an intimate of the Dukes, a close friend of Colonel Andrews, and a man-Friday for the Simmons machine. Their first move was to start a campaign of slander against me, charging that as solicitor I had received improper *scire facias* fees. The very name of "scirefacias" sounded perfectly awful to the average voter, because he didn't understand it. The solicitor's office was on a fee basis, fixed by law for each case disposed óf. When a defendant gave an appearance bond and forfeited it by fleeing the jurisdiction of the court, the compensation to the solicitor for collecting the bond was the same as if the defendant had been convicted on the charge against him. This had been the universal practice with the courts of the state.

During my tenure of office the legislature inserted in the chapter on "School Laws" a paragraph providing a collection fee of 5 per cent on such defaulted bonds, instead of a flat fee. This amendment escaped my attention and the attention of all the clerks of the courts in my district. The practice was for the clerks to make out an itemized statement at the end of each court of the fees due the solicitor and give him a check to cover. When this charge first appeared, I had each clerk go back over his docket and calculate the difference in amount received between the 5 per cent and the usual fees as formerly obtained. The total difference in the vast number of cases disposed of amounted to $345, which the clerks, through mistake, had overpaid me. I promptly sent a check to each clerk to cover the difference, but the reflection lost me some votes, for very few of my supporters knew what a *scire facias* fee was or how to answer the charge.

The psychology of the situation was like that of the story told on Colonel Thomas Fuller in Chatham Court, when the judge told him that his case was *coram non judices* and his client must pay the costs. When Colonel Fuller told his former client that the judge had ruled that his case was *coram non judices,* he replied, "Oh hell, if it is in that bad a fix I'll pay the costs and let it drop."

That was the year that Bryan and Taft were opposing candidates for the presidency and when Bryan's reputation was at its lowest political ebb. It was known throughout the district that Bryan and I were personal friends and that he had several times visited in my home. As the district was highly industrial, many worthy Democrats feared Bryan's radicalism and his probable influence over me if I should be elected. Making matters worse, the preceding General Assembly had added Surry County to the district since the last election, with its 1000 Republican majority.

Unmindful of the unholy political alliance opposing my election and throwing discretion to the wind, I led the inter-party fight in my county to select Kitchin delegates to the State Convention. The contest between Kitchin and Craig for governor was spirited and the state convention at Charlotte wrangled over it for nearly a week before the Simmons machine was finally defeated, and Kitchin—the Bryan liberal—was nominated. A majority of the convention was in favor of endorsing Bryan for the presidency, but Senator Simmons opposed it. A debate ensued in which I made a speech favoring sending an instructed Bryan delegation to the national convention, which was done, and ex-Governor Glenn was chosen to make a speech seconding his nomination at Denver.

In the face of all these powerful forces and handicaps, neither I nor any of my friends ever contemplated my defeat. I was so cocksure that I didn't canvass the district or spend a dollar for organization purposes.

But my enemies had silently and skillfully done their work,

and when the 50,000 votes were counted, I had lost by the slim margin of 248 votes. My chagrin was increased by the distress manifested by so many friends. I had resigned the solicitorship, which I had held so long, and had surprisingly lost the election to Congress, both within a few months. The results were to prove a test of my fortitude and ability to take it standing up, and at the same time a challenge for my future.

16

The Hour of Decision

THE week following my defeat for Congress, I joined J. F. Jordan, an experienced huntsman, and a party of choice friends on a week's camping trip to Manchester for fox hunting and fishing. For a number of years we had annually enjoyed these hunts which were entirely unorthodox in both their preparation and performance.

Jordan owned about thirty thousand acres of cut-over land in the sandhills country between Fayetteville and Pinehurst, which after the sawmills finished with it was left a barren waste, but abounded in gray fox, deer, turkeys, and lakes. Manchester, the camp site, was a wayside station located on the Cape Fear & Yadkin Valley Railroad eighty miles south of Greensboro. The arrangements for the outing consisted of attaching a box car to the rear of the jerkwater passenger train and loading it with hounds and saddle horses, provender for the horses, provisions for the men, and a good Negro cook with helpers. Near the Manchester station was a row of abandoned sawmill shacks which were crudely fitted up as a camp.

At the crack of dawn each morning we had breakfast, mounted our horses, and loosed the hounds. Frequently they would in a few minutes strike the trail of a fox that had been prowling around the camp the night before. The terrain was ideally suited for this kind of hunting, with its long bays of gallberry bushes growing along the creeks and branches, which afforded a dense cover for the fox as he ran sometimes for several hours up and down for miles with the hounds in hot pursuit. The old abandoned logging roads made it easy for the horsemen to stay close to the hounds and revel in the music of the pack without a skip in the chase. Occasionally the wily fox would try to trick the hounds by slipping out of cover and racing for a mile or so across the sandhills to another bay—which rarely saved the fox but gave the hunters an opportunity to follow closely and see the hounds work. It was counted a poor hunt when fewer than two or three foxes were tailed each day. The day's fox hunt over, some of the campers would go fishing—some to hunt deer. Jordan, who was a crack shot, would frequently bring in an old buck.

At night after the others had retired, I sat alone and watched the embers slowly die, even as my political ambition was fading into dust. I reviewed every important event in my life, beginning with my election as solicitor, and appraised each one to determine the wisdom or the folly of my decisions. At the threshold of my political career I had refused to accept railroad passes as a state official in violation of law and against the public policy of the state. This alone had cost me far more than the 250 votes needed to elect me to Congress. I still did not see how a conscientious public official could have done otherwise, and I did not regret the decision. I recalled that not joining the Simmons machine had invited its opposition to my political ambitions and lay like a lion across my path to any future preferment in public life. For ten years I had observed its ruthless methods, its subservience to railroad dictation, and its reliance upon favor-seeking big business for financial support to keep it going. I catalogued in my remembrance that wise old friends had warned against my becoming a candidate for Congress, particularly ex-Governor Thomas J. Jarvis, who like a father said, "Brooks, don't make the mistake of going to Congress. It will spoil your career at the bar and bring you little happiness." Likewise, Captain E. S. Parker, a distinguished old lawyer, sitting in his law office in Graham, said, "Brooks, if you want to go to Congress, I will support you, but at your age, with your aptitude for the law, I think it a serious mistake."

But disregarding these sage admonitions, I accepted the nomination. Before the election day I was faced with another decision. R. J. Reynolds, founder of the Reynolds Tobacco Company, had invited me to become chief counsel for his company. He offered me a magnificent salary for those days, and told me he would make me rich by financing the purchase of stock in his company then comparatively in its infancy. But the glamor of a political future was overweaning, and I declined the offer.

With the office of solicitor gone, defeated for Congress, and the one opportunity of becoming a multimillionaire counsel for a great industrial enterprise gone, the future looked gloomy. But on the other side of life's ledger I calmly recounted that I still had youth, health, courage, and the will to win, and this inspired the resolve to return to my first love, the law, and enthrone it as the mistress of my life.

A few years later, Jordan sold the boundary of land where we had camped to Percy Rockefeller for a permanent hunting preserve. Some miles north of our old camp Rockefeller built a clubhouse, attractive winter cottages, and stables for his string of fine hunters. He named this settlement "Overhills," which is still in use. Each fall he invited me and a few others of the old guard fox hunters as his guests for a week.

In 1917 the announcement came from the War Department that this large boundary of land would be taken over for a permanent camp site. This greatly disturbed Rockefeller, and he set about to satisfy the government that he could furnish enough of his forty thousand acres to serve its purpose and leave his settlement and adjacent boundary untouched. Some months before, Newton D. Baker, Secretary of War, had come to North Carolina on a speaking engagement and was entertained for a couple of days at my home. Rockefeller, learning of my personal acquaintance with the Secretary, asked me to arrange a conference with him and to present the matter, as I was familiar with the geography of the locality. The request for a conference was granted. Rockefeller, Everit Macy, an interested friend, and I were cordially received and I explained fully the factual situation, pointing out that a little river ran directly through the middle of the boundary and that the twenty thousand acres lying south of this stream was admirably suited for the purposes desired. I suggested that he have the government engineers survey the situation and if they found the indicated acreage south of the river adequate for its needs it would accommodate Rockefeller and his friends by leaving intact half of the game preserve and the extensive improvements, which in no event could be of any value or service to the army. The Secretary promptly accepted the suggestion, and later advised me that the government needed and would take only the land south of the river.

As a result, our old camp site and the scenes of many a fox hunt are occupied by the great Camp Bragg, where during World Wars I and II tens upon tens of thousands troops were serviced for action, while across the little river to the north, "Overhills" camp remains a haven of pleasure in times of peace.

17

A Lady, A Library, and A Lake

WHEN I came back to the office I was surprised to find that so many of my friends regarded my defeat for Congress as a blessing in disguise. A seat in Congress then paid only $5,000 a year, which made it impossible to save anything from the salary. I had already a few regular clients, and as I was free from any political ambitions, others soon began to engage my services, so that the first year I collected more than the congressional salary amounted to. Through the events narrated in the next chapter, I had already become counsel for the North State Fire Insurance Company, the Dixie Fire Insurance Company, the Security Life & Trust Company, and the Postal Telegraph Company. I soon discovered that clients did not want counsel who were active in politics, and my time was completely engaged by old and new clients. I was frequently employed in important cases in Rockingham, Caswell, and Alamance counties in addition to my home county of Guilford.

In 1910 I was married to Miss Helen Higbie of New Jersey. Throughout the years, in sunshine and shadow, we have shared each other's joys and borne each other's sorrows, and she has ever been a perfect companion and mate. As Sir Walter Raleigh wrote of his wife, "She has ever been 'my heart's ease.'"

From our union came three sons—Aubrey Lee, who at twenty died from the results of an automobile accident received while he was a student at the University of North Carolina in Chapel Hill; Thornton Higbie, who now is a partner in my law firm; and James Taylor, who is a physician in Greensboro.

In 1912 Irving Park, two miles north of town, was opened, a golf course laid out, and a clubhouse built in its center. We acquired an eight-acre tract of land fronting the golf course, across from the club, and built our home in the midst of a grove of stately white oaks, lofty pines, and a profusion of dogwood. It was among the first homes built in Irving Park.

Fortune and finance now happily combined to bring to fruition a dream of my boyhood. In youth I had looked with admiration at the stately ante-bellum Georgian mansions in Virginia and North Carolina, and wistfully longed that I might some day own one. My ideal was Mount Vernon, but to reproduce it in a house with modern conveniences and improvements without sacrificing its architectural simplicity and charm was a task for which at first I was unprepared. In the front of our home stands a stately tulip poplar, the largest in the county, and so we named it "Poplar Hall."

Through the years we have accumulated a large library, which is a constant source of pleasure. In an old English classic I once read that every gentleman should possess a lady, a library and a lake. I had the lady and the library, so why not a lake to complete my trinity of delights? The lake was added in 1927. There may be a difference of opinion as to the charms of a lady or the pleasures of a selected library, but no lover of outdoor sports will deny the joy of a well-stocked lake conveniently located.

In Piedmont North Carolina it is difficult to secure a large private lake fed exclusively by spring branches and free from discoloration, on account of the constant erosion of red clay soil from surrounding hills. After much exploring I fortunately found such a site twelve miles north of Greensboro, and built a dam impounding forty acres of clear water entirely surrounded by woods and fed by spring branches. I stocked it with small-mouth bass, bream, and crappie and built a cabin overlooking it. For twenty years now it has been a source of pleasure to us and our friends. As this is written, at seventy-eight I still enjoy luring the game fish with a fly-rod and my wife at seventy swims with ease from one side of the lake to the other. I very naturally named it for her—"Lake Helen."

In 1912 I joined the First Presbyterian Church, the oldest religious institution in Greensboro. From a small village church it has grown with the community until now it is regarded as the oldest and most prominent church in the General Assembly of the Southern Presbyterian Churches. I was elected a deacon in 1923 and a trustee in 1933, which positions I still hold. By the late twenties the congregation had become so big and the membership so large that it became necessary to build a larger edifice to seat a thousand Sunday school children and fifteen hundred members. A building committee was appointed, of which I became a member of the finance committee. The new structure was completed in 1929 and represented a total cost of $750,000. It became necessary also to borrow $450,000, which we found difficult to do. At that time I was a member of the finance committee of the Jefferson Standard Life Insurance Company and personally secured its approval of the loan. The church is now entirely free of debt and we have a membership of twenty-five hundred.

This is recorded as a matter of history, but I lay no claim to being a professional religionist. My connection with the church has been solely to acknowledge the existence of God and a belief in the saving grace of Jesus Christ. I have never sought, directly or indirectly, to use my connection with the church to promote social intercourse, political favor, or financial opportunity.

18

The Hartford of the South

THE beginning of the twentieth century brought to Greensboro new life and opened up new vistas. Religious and educational influences had long made it a desirable place in which to live. Emphasis had always been placed upon its church life and upon good educational facilities for children. But now a new generation was coming to the front, one which recognized that the town was deficient in industry. Forward-looking young men, forgetting the dead past, were now bent on helping to build a new South. They became critical, pointing out that the South's economic set-up was totally out of balance, and that it was buying in the North nearly every article of consumption not produced locally on farms and plantations. As this younger generation became more and more economic-minded and trade-conscious, they revolted against the heavy insurance premiums paid for both life and fire protection to Eastern companies, and demanded that Southern companies be organized to keep this money at home. The heavy drain on the South, not only in insurance but in many other fields, was pictured in a cartoon of a cow feeding in the South, with her milk bag in the North, giving all her milk to feed the economic life of that section.

In those days there was little state control or regulation of insurance companies, and the high rates charged made the business very profitable. As a result of all this, Greensboro became so insurance-minded that in a period of twelve years from 1900 to 1912 local groups organized four life insurance companies and six fire insurance companies, all with home offices in Greensboro. Such a daring and remarkable achievement for a town of its size attracted national attention, and Greensboro was called "The Hartford of the South." The forerunner and father of this new form of enterprise in both fire and life companies was A. W. McAlister. He was a wiry little Scotchman with a good background, and a fine character, well educated, ambitious, and industrious. Operating an agency for foreign life insurance and fire insurance companies, he saw the big profits for the underwriters and the opportunity for such home companies. He organized over a period of years the first fire companies in Greensboro—four in all—and in 1903 he organized the Pilot Life Insurance Company. McAlister was public-spirited and took the lead in organizing the Greensboro Country Club, Irving Park, and later Sedgefield and its country club.

In 1906 the North State Fire Insurance Company was organized and I became its general counsel, director, and a member of its finance committee. Two years later the same group, joined by a number of prominent business men throughout the state, organized the Dixie Fire Insurance Company, with a paid-in capital of $500,000 and a surplus of $250,000. This was the largest of all the local companies and one of the largest in the South. It did business throughout the nation. I drew its charter and was elected a director, member of the executive committee, and general counsel. The business of the Dixie Company increased so rapidly that the stockholders of the North State Company agreed to merge with it so as to provide a larger capital and surplus, which would allow it to write a still greater volume of business. There was then no law in North Carolina authorizing the merger of corporations. I was assigned the difficult task of joining them together so that it would stick and pass the scrutiny of the insurance commissioners of the various states, from New York to California, in which the company was doing business. What I joined together no man has put asunder, but it was a ticklish performance.

In 1901 ten prominent Greensboro citizens organized a mutual life insurance company and named it the Security Life and Annuity Company. They deposited with the state insurance commissioner their respective notes for $10,000 each as a guarantee of the company's faithful performance. I became general counsel for this company. The dealers in this undertaking were George A. Grimsley, J. Van Lindley, J. W. Scott, P. H. Hanes, C. C. Taylor, and others. A few years later a small group led by J. E. Latham and R. P. Richardson, organized the Greensboro Life Insurance Company with a capital of $146,000.

In 1909, P. D. Gold and Charles Gold organized the Jefferson Standard Life Insurance Company in Raleigh with a capital of $250,000 and a like amount of surplus. By 1912 it ran into difficulty as the result of having depleted its surplus by writing too much business, and the stockholders declined to put up additional capital and surplus. By this time the Greensboro Life was in a similar situation. The Security Life and Trust Company, being a mutual company without capital requirements, had grown by leaps and bounds. But realizing that it would hurt all the insurance companies to have the Greensboro Life and the Jefferson Standard Life fold up, George A. Grimsley, president of the Security Life and Trust, which had a larger business on its books than either of the other two companies, conceived the idea of merging the three companies. Thus, by his putting in his mutual business and assets, the necessity of adding additional capital would be avoided if the consolidated company was prudently managed. As counsel for the Security Life and Trust Company I took part in the negotiations and conducted the legal aspects of the merger, which resulted in bringing the Jefferson Standard Life Insurance Company to Greensboro and using its name for the consolidated companies.

As a result of the merger, the combined capital account of the three companies was fixed at $250,000, and the surplus account was carried at $384,989. A large number of prominent business men throughout the state were chosen as associates and, with this set-up, the company prospered greatly. George A. Grimsley was naturally voted president and I was elected a director, a member of the finance committee, and general counsel of the company. The rapid growth of the company required increased legal services, which in turn required my engaging associates to assist in looking after the business. The effect of all this tended to make me a one-client lawyer which I had always sought to avoid.

In 1917 it became apparent that we should have an office building suitable for a growing institution, and the directors delegated me a committee of one to secure a site. I began negotiations with the county commissioners, who had announced that they intended to remove the County Court House situated on the public square of the city. The sale was consummated and the company purchased the old Court House and lot for $171,000. We later constructed the present Jefferson Standard Building—a magnificent seventeen-story structure. I was appointed a member of a committee of four to construct the building. It is a credit to the city and a monument to the company.

After the merger of the North State Fire Insurance Company with the Dixie, we thought it advisable to select a new president and I was delegated to interview Harry R. Bush, then an officer of the American Insurance Company of Newark, New Jersey. He became our new president and continued in that office until his death. He was an experienced insurance man of fine ability and an addition to the city. In 1928 we exchanged all of our stock in the Dixie Fire Insurance Company for stock in the American Insurance Company of Newark, and this arrangement continued until recently, when the Dixie became absorbed by the American. It is a matter of pride and profit to me that I have been continually retained as counsel for the Dixie and American for forty years and at a substantial salary.

A few years after the merger of the life insurance companies, I was elected a member of the Association of General Counsel of the leading life insurance companies in the United States. These counsel met twice a year—in December at New York and mid-year in different parts of the country. One year, upon my invitation, they held their meeting in Greensboro. For fifteen years I regularly attended their meetings. However, they grew increasingly irksome because nothing but technical insurance law was ever discussed. At these meetings the counsel referred to themselves as "kept lawyers"—an appellation which I inherently resented.

When the three companies were merged, I purchased a substantial block of stock in the new company. I have never purchased a share of stock in it since. For the twenty years I remained with the company, many opportunities were offered to purchase stock in the company from distressed stockholders and innocent ones who were not in a position to know its true value. I was financially able to increase my stock holdings, but I was an officer of the company and a member of the finance committee, and when I accepted these positions I regarded them as a sacred trust to look after the stockholders' interests in the company and not to use the trust position to make money on the side at the expense of unsuspecting stockholders.

In Canada it is made a crime for an officer or a director to purchase stock of his own company unless it is listed on the stock exchange. There should be such a law in North Carolina. When I left the company in 1932 the business in force amounted to $358,000,000, and it was so well established that nothing could prevent its continued growth, as subsequent events have shown. The Pilot Life Insurance Company, in the meantime, had grown to considerable size and had built a splendid office building at Sedgefield. When the opportunity came, we purchased substantially all of the stock of the Pilot, but it has maintained a separate existence and conducts a growing business on its own account. This again added more work for the general counsel of the Jefferson Standard.

The management of the Jefferson grew impatient at doing a regular life insurance business and began speculating by buying up hotels and other business properties in various states and lending large sums of money to individual borrowers and investing in other like accounts. This practice grew increasingly distasteful to me, for I felt that an insurance company should not hazard its fortunes by engaging in speculation of any kind. J. E. Latham, who had helped build the company agreed with me, and we emphasized these views to the management. In addition to all this, it developed that the company was borrowing from the Reconstruction Finance Corporation $1,400,000, and, in order to boost the company's statement, the dividend to policy holders was reduced by something over $500,000. We were told that since the management had been buying up stock on credit, it was necessary for the company to declare a dividend, which in fact amounted to using borrowed money to pay stock dividends by the company that had lost money that year.

At the annual meeting of the stockholders in 1932, by the use of proxies quietly collected, Latham and I were voted out as directors. It did not greatly disturb me because I preferred the general practice of the law, but I regretted it on Latham's account, for he had taken great pride in the company and it wounded his feelings to be thus summarily voted out. George A. Holderness, who was a charter member of the Jefferson Standard, a director and vice president, entertained similar views, and at once disposed of all of his stock in the company and retired.

At this meeting I asked the management who was advising this course of conduct, and was told that they were acting under the advice of one of my law partners. Immediately after the meeting was over I went to my office, called in all of my partners, and dissolved the partnership, an act which was long overdue. I moved my offices to the Southeastern Building and took with me as partners, E. S. Parker, Jr., and W. H. Holderness. Clients in all walks of life came to us, and through the years we have done a growing law business. The firm now consists of Brooks, McLendon, Brim and Holderness and my son Thornton, with three legal associates, which, incidentally, allows me time to take long vacations and to write these memoirs.

Since the above was written there has occurred a convulsion in the Jefferson Standard Life Insurance Company. The President, Ralph Price, who was selected as president of the company, by his father, Julian Price, was unceremoniously disposed of in May, 1950, and, so far as the public knew, without cause. Howard Holderness, a brother of one of my partners, an outsider, was elected in his stead. Holderness has youth and ability and is by nature a conservative in business. It is to be hoped that the company will quit its speculative practices of long standing and devote its energies strictly to the insurance business for which it was organized. The company now owns the control of the leading bank in Greensboro, which is bad for the city, the bank, and the company.

It also owns a radio station in Charlotte and one in Greensboro, which is no part of legitimate insurance. The Jefferson Standard Life Insurance Company owns all the stock of the Pilot Life Insurance Company, and the combined insurance in the two companies is now over one and one-half billion dollars. I think it high time that these companies get in line with the great insurance companies of the nation and let the "shoemaker stick to his last."

19

Unusual Trials in Federal Courts

ONE day in 1913 a distinguished looking gentleman called at my office, introduced himself as "Shaw," and said that he wished to employ me to defend a case brought against him in the state court at Salisbury and removed to the Federal court at Greensboro for trial. I asked him where he was from. "I am a native of Iowa," he replied, "where I was once governor. Afterwards I lived in Washington, where I was secretary of the Treasury, but now my home is in Philadelphia." "So this is the Honorable Leslie M. Shaw," I deferentially observed. He gave me a history of his troubles, which were, briefly, that as head of a trust company in Philadelphia he had visited Salisbury and entered into contractual relations with certain parties for the purchase of a local utility. Afterwards a serious dispute arose which involved questions of veracity and fraudulent representation. He had declined to carry through the trade, and was sued for $150,000 damages and charged with wilful fraud. I never knew how he happened to employ me, but I cheerfully undertook his defense.

We both realized the gravity of the case, especially the element involving fraud, which made it a matter for a jury. He was conscious of no wrong-doing, but was extremely nervous over what a Southern Democratic jury might do to a Northern Republican Yankee—evidence or no evidence. I assured him that there was no such danger from our juries, and that upon the evidence and the law they should—and I felt would—acquit him.

The case was set for trial early in January, and to make sure of our readiness, he, accompanied by his daughter, came down ahead of time. My wife invited them for dinner on New Year's Eve, when an embarrassing, yet amusing situation developed. Our servants were dependable Negroes, but my dear old father had given them too much eggnog, and when time for dinner arrived the cook was drunk, the waitress asleep, and the butler in the cellar singing, "Nearer, My God, to Thee."

As the trial approached, I observed that Shaw's increasing nervousness was making him more talkative. Fearing that he might make a bad impression on the court and jury by appearing too shrewd, I cautioned him when on the witness stand to answer the questions of counsel simply and directly and not try to make a speech to the jury. "You are no doubt a better lawyer than I am, but you can't try your own case before a North Carolina jury as well as I can." He responded graciously, and made an admirable witness. The jury, after a two days' hearing, promptly answered all the issues in his favor. The plaintiffs carried the case to the Circuit Court of Appeals at Richmond. After a jury's verdict we felt little concern, but nevertheless it was pleasing to observe on the wall of one of the judges' chambers a portrait of "Leslie M. Shaw, Secretary of the Treasury of the United States."

During Theodore Roosevelt's second term, he went on the rampage against senators' and congressmen's appearing as counsel before governmental departments in Washington in violation of an old statute long overlooked. The attorney general was directed to institute indictments against all offenders, expose, and convict them. Caught in this dragnet among the notables was Spence Blackburn, Republican congressman from North Carolina. Blackburn was a tall, handsome young fellow, with personality plus. He had married a socialite in Washington and had bought a home in Greensboro, even though it was outside his mountain district. The specific charges against him were that he had collected compensation from some of his constituents for helping them out of trouble with certain departments in Washington.

When he engaged me to represent him, he requested that I go to Washington to consult some of his associates in Congress, especially his friend, Speaker Joseph G. Cannon. This was an interesting experience for me. Of course none of the congressmen approved of the prosecution, but there was little help they could give. My visit to Uncle Joe Cannon was worth the price of the trip. He was born in Guilford County and attended for a few years the Quaker School, New Garden, now Guilford College, before his parents moved to Illinois. I found him an interesting old cuss and full of venom against "the damn upstart at the other end of Pennsylvania Avenue." Here was the man who for so many years had dominated the House, and they called him Joe. "That fellow," said he, "would send if he could every senator and congressman to the penitentiary who opposes his Rough Rider methods. One of the troubles up here," he went on, "is there are too many representatives without guts, who keep their ears so close to the ground that crickets get in them."

For personal reasons and to avoid political implications, Judge Boyd and District Attorney A. E. Holton both disqualified themselves from taking part in the trial. This resulted in the attorney general's designating Judge Guy D. Goff, senior Circuit Court judge of the fourth circuit, to preside at the trial, and Colonel Anderson, district attorney from Richmond, Virginia, to prosecute the case. Judge Goff, who later became senator from West Virginia, was regarded as an eminent jurist, and a perfectly fair trial was assured. From the outset of the trial, the name of "Ace Dinkins," a Government star witness, was repeatedly mentioned, but the evidence closed without the Government's putting him on the stand. In my closing argument to the jury, after stressing the Government's failure to call their principal witness, a bit of humor was injected when, turning to the prosecutor, I demanded, "Where is your Ace?" "Lost in the shuffle," the prosecutor replied. Then turning to the jury I jokingly said, "Yes, gentlemen, the Government's Ace was lost in the shuffle, and it played the deuce."

Blackburn was promptly acquitted.

One day a case came to me that was weird almost beyond belief. The newspapers one morning reported in startling headlines that the post office in near-by Kernersville had been robbed the night before and that the robber had been captured and lodged in the county jail. A few days later the sheriff of the county phoned that a prisoner wished to consult me. Arriving at the jail I was taken to a cell and there met the accused, who looked more like a gentleman than a criminal. He was tall, well-dressed, dignified in appearance, and apparently well past middle age. Opening the conversation, he referred to himself as the "old man" and addressed me as "Senator," saying he wished to employ me to represent the "old man" in the charges against him for robbing the post office. We agreed upon a fee of $500, which he said would be paid in a few days by a man who would call at my office. He expressed the wish not to discuss the case until the fee was paid.

Some days later a nice looking stranger walked into my office and asked if this was Mr. Brooks who was counsel for the man charged with robbing the Kernersville post office, omitting to mention the man's name. When I replied that I was, he drew from his pocket five one-hundred-dollar bills, laid them on my desk, and started out.

"Wait a minute," said I, "and tell me something about this man, who he is, where he came from and what is his defense?"

Calmly looking me in the eye, he replied, "Your fee is five hundred dollars, there is the money; I have no further business with you. Good day." And he walked out.

Strangely I could never get the "old man" to discuss the facts of his case. Unperturbed, he would say, "Senator, let's await developments and I will go into the details when it becomes necessary."

The developments soon came, but from the outside, when the Associated Press broke the news from Chicago that a notoriously known post office robber had been captured and was in jail in Greensboro awaiting trial in the Federal court. Quickly followed the announcement that the Department of Justice had called a special term of Federal court to be held in Salisbury to try this man, and that post office inspectors from different sections of the nation would attend the trial. My position as counsel was an anomalous one. The press and the public were agog over the case, but my client kept silent in all languages. When I cautioned him that I could not intelligently try his case unless I knew the facts upon which he relied as a defense, he calmly assured me that he quite understood that fact; that he would go into the matter after the court met in Salisbury and he knew the witness the Government had to testify against him.

Thus suspended in thin air, I awaited developments upon the convening of court—a most amazing situation. The Federal judge and district attorney and their retinue of witnesses assembled in Salisbury for the trial of this single case. In a conference with my client, who had been removed to the Salisbury jail on the morning that the court opened, he said "Senator, the government is relying for conviction solely upon the testimony of a boy who was with the 'old man' on the fateful night. This boy got into trouble because he had no sense of courses and distances; but he cannot testify against the 'old man' because he is an ex-convict, and having served a term in the Leavenworth Federal Penitentiary for a felony, under the law his testimony is not admissible."

Both the fact and the law were news to me and I at once interviewed Holton, the United States district attorney, who admitted that the boy was his chief witness but that he knew nothing of his being an ex-convict and would check it up. Upon investigation he informed me that my client's statement was true and that he could not use him as a witness in the case. (The law has since been changed.) This created an embarrassing situation for the court which had met specially to try this case and had brought post office detectives as witnesses from Chicago, New York, and Washington to show this man to be a notorious robber of post offices, who had previously served a prison term for a similar offense.

When the court convened, the "old man" pleaded not guilty, which left the Government helpless to proceed and threatened to break up the court, force the district attorney to find other evidence if he could, and start all over again.

The district attorney then approached me with the proposition that if the defendant would plead guilty he would recommend that the judge give him a light sentence. I agreed to consult with my client and the court took a recess for this purpose. To my surprise several impressive looking gentlemen whom I had noticed in the courtroom came over and greeted my client in a most cordial manner, like old friends. "What does this mean?" I asked him when we reached a conference room. With a complacent smile he said, "Senator, those men are old friends of mine from Chicago, where I live. They are post office inspectors and detectives, but have no ill feeling toward me. As you may understand, they know the "old man's" business and know that he never takes money or anything of financial value from a post office, only government stamps which can be replaced by merely printing more. "About a month ago," said he, "I gave a banquet in Chicago that cost me a thousand dollars, which they attended and we had a jolly time. But you will appreciate that they want to keep their jobs and if even a friend gets too bold and indiscreet and is apprehended, they must enforce the law." When I reported the district attorney's proposal about disposing of his case, a satisfied smile lit up his face, like a cat that had swallowed a canary.

Then followed an illuminating unfolding of his strategy, which he evidently had in mind from the beginning but had never disclosed to his counsel. This is in substance what he lined out, more like a judge than an accused: "Senator, we have now reached the point where I think we can do business with the Government; the officers of the court are embarrassed by the predicament in which they find themselves and are anxious to get rid of the case. If the court is adjourned they will keep me in jail and double their efforts to convict later, and they might get enough evidence to convict the "old man." Let's do some trading. Tell the district attorney we will take eighteen months in the Atlanta Penitentiary and call it a day."

After some backing and filling this was agreed to, and thus ended an actual experience in criminology that was stranger than fiction. Upon my departure the old man ironically said, "Senator, you should have charged me a larger fee for this kind of a case." The suggestion that the fee was too little came too late; however, the observation did serve as a reminder never again so to offend the sensibilities of an important client. I quit the case feeling that Mr. Blackstone's statement, "A man who appears for himself has a fool for a client," is not always true.

One day the collector of internal revenue, who was stationed in Raleigh, caused a mild sensation when he announced that he intended to collect an income tax on the salaries of the judges in the state. The salaries of the judges, from the Supreme Court down, were comparatively small and they had never been required to pay income taxes. The judges of course, opposed the idea and employed me to represent them.

The State Constitution provided that the salaries of the judges should not be decreased during their term of office and they were elected for eight-year terms. The theory of the constitutional provision was that no legislature should have the right to abolish the office or reduce the income of judges during their term of office. I brought an action in Guilford County enjoining the Collector from levying and collecting the tax. It was a novel suit of first impression in North Carolina. Upon investigation, I found that the Supreme Court of the United States had passed upon a similar question and that a few states had construed a similar constitutional provision. I found that the Constitution of the United States had a like provision and that all these courts had held that any attempt to disregard this inhibition was unconstitutional. The case was argued in the Superior Court and it upheld our contention. The Collector appealed to the Supreme Court, where, in an exhaustive opinion, the lower court's opinion was affirmed. The judges offered to pay me for my services but I declined to accept any compensation.

Some years later, the salaries of judges became subject to the income tax.

20

North Carolina Public Service Company v. Duke Power Company

IT IS A curious and interesting fact that some of the most important events in our lives have their origin in remote circumstances to which, at the time, we attach little importance. Such was my connection with the North Carolina Public Service Company and its long and bitter litigation with James B. Duke and his Southern Power Company.

W. N. Coler and the Hole Brothers of New York owned the North Carolina Public Service Company, which operated the street railway and electric lighting plants in Greensboro, High Point, Salisbury, Spencer, and East Spencer.

The Chamber of Commerce in Greensboro gave a dinner to these gentlemen and some visiting bankers. I presided, and there for the first time I met Bird Coler. We later met on the train to New York, and during the conversation I remarked that I was on my way to Hartford. He told me of an engagement he had there later in the week for a joint debate with Dr. Lun on Socialism, before a Get-Together Club, and asked me to attend as his guest. It proved to be an interesting experience, as I knew little of Socialism. Coler opened with a well prepared address which he delivered from manuscript. In reply, Dr. Lun, an accomplished speaker, outclassed Coler as a debater. He made little of the Bible and slurred the Constitution and the flag. By the time he had finished I was outraged, and at the conclusion of the debate when the chairman asked if I would not like to speak, I promptly said "Yes."

I began by saying that I was from the South, where we had tried to secede from the Union, as they had once tried to do, but we were now in the Union where we proposed to stay; that Dr. Lun's theories were revolutionary to me, and un-American. I then proceeded to deliver a eulogy on the Bible, the Constitution, and our national flag. The audience responded and the press next morning featured my remarks. The result was that Coler employed me as general counsel for his company, and later made me vice president.

The company had entered into a contract with J. B. Duke, owner of the Southern Power Company, to purchase electric power and current to supply its requirements for the cities of Greensboro, High Point, Salisbury, and Spencer, and their inhabitants. This contract carried a provision that the Public Service Company should scrap its steam plants, which had theretofore generated their current. Its contract was expiring in 1914 and when a renewal was asked, Duke's company demanded a large increase in price per kilowatt hour for its current, much above the charge Duke was making for current sold to the Southern Public Utilities Company owned by him and operating in the adjoining towns of Winston-Salem, Reidsville, and others. Our company was in a dilemma, as there was no other available source of power, and the rate proposed, if agreed to, meant ultimate bankruptcy.

When the Public Service Company demurred, Duke demanded that the increased rates be accepted or he would discontinue service. In the face of this arbitrary demand, I advised the company to try and sell the property to Duke and get out of his clutches. Charles Hole, the president, and I went to New York to see Duke. He blandly said the company was over-bonded and that the common stock was not worth the $25 per share we asked, and in fact had no value, and that he would pay nothing for it.

The only resource left was to resort to the court. I warned the directors that a suit meant a battle to the death, that Duke was ruthless and his monopoly in the tobacco business had been accomplished by destroying weaker competitors, and that he was going to seek to acquire a monopoly in both wholesale and retail distribution of current in Western North Carolina, as he had done in the world monopoly of the tobacco trade, by means of the American Tobacco Trust.

As bearing upon the methods of the man we were dealing with, I called to their attention that the Supreme Court of the United States, in an opinion dissolving the Tobacco Trust a few years before, had charged Duke by name with being guilty, for seventeen years, of conscious wrong-doing, and that there was no evidence he had either repented or reformed. Still I gave it as my opinion that if they had the guts to fight it out in the courts we could whip him and save the company.

The directors instructed me to proceed, which I promptly did by filing a bill in equity asking the court to enjoin the Southern Power Company from cutting off current and putting the cities in darkness. The material facts relied upon were comparatively simple, and were not denied. The bill alleged that the Southern Power Company was a foreign corporation, which North Carolina had licensed to do business in the state and had given the right of eminent domain; that it had filed with the

State Corporation Commission a declaration denying that the commissioners had any right to fix or regulate the rates it charged for current to said consumers; that as a result it arbitrarily discriminated by charging different rates to various users of its current, and particularly grossly favored the Southern Public Utilities Company, a subsidiary engaged in operating and retailing current in other cities just as the Public Service Company was doing. The bill did not ask the court to fix the rate to be charged, but prayed that the company be required to continue to serve as it served other similar companies in the state, without discrimination in either rates or service.

In its answer the company denied being a public service corporation, and asserted that it owed no duty to the plaintiff, that the courts had no jurisdiction or control over its business, and that it was at liberty to sell or refuse to sell to anyone, as it chose. Such a position taken by a foreign corporation, whose very existence depended upon the grace of the state, was to me the very epitome of insolence, and I never doubted that the courts would stop Duke in his ruthless course. But it took six years of strenuous litigation in both the state and Federal courts to do it.

The defendants' first move was to demur to the allegation of the bill, which had the effect in law of admitting the truth of the facts alleged. The lower court overruled the demurrer, and the defendants appealed from this ruling to the Supreme Court of the state. That court sustained the ruling below and in an elaborate opinion said it was a case of first importance to the people of the state; that the power company's position was a challenge to the right of the state to regulate the rates and services of public utilities companies; and that such a position was contrary to public policy and indefensible in a court of justice. The opinion pointed out that J. B. Duke, who owned the Power Company, was the same Duke who organized the American Tobacco Company, which the courts had dissolved as a criminal trust, and that he was employing in the operation of this power company methods of ruthlessly destroying competition similar to those he had employed in building the Tobacco Trust.

Notwithstanding this decision, a brilliant staff of lawyers, Edward T. Cansler, Judge Osborne and W. S. O'B. Robinson of Charlotte, Judges Bynum and Strudwick of Greensboro and Richard V. Lindabury of New Jersey, carried the case from the State Supreme Court to the Federal District Court, the Circuit Court of Appeals, and finally to the Supreme Court of the United States. I had associated with me John W. Davis of New York. Mr. Davis appeared on the morning of the argument wearing a cutaway coat. I remarked that he had left me wearing a black sack coat. He replied, "When I appear before this august court, I always try to protect my gable end."

During my argument before the Supreme Court of the United States, Chief Justice Taft said, "Mr. Brooks, I see from the record that this Power Company is a foreign corporation which your state permits to do business in and enjoy the right of eminent domain. Hasn't the Supreme Court of the State ruled against this Power Company on all of its contentions here"? My reply was, "Yes, Your Honor, not once but twice, and the Circut Court of Appeals has likewise done so; yet after six years of litigation it is here still resisting the mandates of the court. I am persuaded that nothing will stop it unless this court speaks to it in a language it can understand." Before the argument ended, Justice Oliver Wendell Holmes in his rasping voice interrupted to say to counsel for the Power Company that the suit should not have been brought into that court.

Of course it should never have been necessary to institute the suit in the first instance, if the State Corporation Commission had possessed the courage and disposition to regulate the service and rates of this defiant monopoly.

It was not long thereafter that Barstow & Company of New York, dealers in public utilities, approached the Public Service Company with a proposition to buy its common stock at $75 per share—the same stock that Duke had pronounced worthless. We suspected that Duke inspired this offer, but as the price was reasonable, the offer was accepted. In a comparatively short time Duke's Southern Public Utilities Company turned up as the owner of the company, after paying (as was reported) a handsome profit to the intermediary.

When the courts dismissed every contention of the Power Company and laid down the law governing its operation, Duke made a flank movement designed to destroy the Public Service Company, notwithstanding the court's decision in its favor. He had his wholly-owned Southern Public Utilities Company apply to the City Council of Greensboro for a franchise to furnish it and its inhabitants with current and power. The City Council submitted the question to a vote of the people, who overwhelmingly killed it. Defeated in court and hemmed off by the people of the city, Duke reversed his contention that his Southern Power Company was not a public service company, and had it file a petition asking the State Corporation Commission to allow it to breach all existing contracts with consumers of current, and increase its then existing rates.

Together with many other consumers of power, we appeared before the commissioners and opposed the increase in rates. Duke appeared before the commission with a battery of high-powered lawyers and experts. When it became evident that the commission was going to grant the petition, I insisted that their decree include a mandate that the company be required to serve the Public Service Company upon the same conditions as it was serving other like companies in the state and put a stop to the useless litigation. The Power Company objected, and the spineless commission declined to do it, expressly disregarding the decision of the Supreme Court of the state. I was so outraged at this action that I said to the commissioners, if they had no regard for the decision of the Supreme Court of the state, I intended getting a decision from Chief Justice Taft of the Supreme Court of the United States, where the case was then pending, that there was no justification or excuse for the Power Company's arbitrary course in declining to serve the Public Service Company.

In the light of Chief Justice Taft's remarks to me at the hearing, I took particular pleasure in handing a copy of that court's opinion to A. J. Maxwell, the dominant member of the Corporation Commission, with the statement that it was a pity his commission would not enforce the law of the state as declared by its Supreme Court but forced litigants to go to the Federal courts to protect their rights.

The Supreme Court, in a brief opinion, wrote *finis* to this long litigation.

21

From the Sublime to the Sordid

From my earliest boyhood on the Person County plantation, I had heard the returning Confederate soldiers from the battlefields of Virginia tell in glowing terms of the beauty of the Shenandoah Valley, its undulating acres, its vast fields of golden wheat, corn, and oats, its miles of pastures on which well-bred cattle and horses grazed in blue grass and timothy up to their bellies, its crystal streams, and the chain of Blue Ridge mountains in the far distance extending its entire length like Heaven's curtain to shield and protect this Garden of Eden.

In the summer of 1920 an opportunity came for me and my family to see this valley in full dress. We entered it from Roanoke by automobile, on our way to Bay Head on the New Jersey coast, where my wife's family spent their summers. Taking it leisurely along the narrow, curving turnpike roads, we enjoyed every mile of it. At Lexington we lunched and visited the home of Stonewall Jackson, one of the world's great military leaders, and saw the statue of General Lee and the mounted skeleton of his beloved horse Traveller. To me, Lee's statue is one of the most awe-inspiring pieces of sculpture I have ever seen. The artist has so arranged one of Lee's hands that you instinctively feel he might at any moment raise it for a kindly handshake.

Night overtook us at Mount Jackson, where at a small hotel we stayed until morning. Strolling along the streets of this tiny village under the shadow of Mount Jackson, I saw a white-bearded old gentleman sitting in front of a one-room office, smoking his pipe in perfect contentment. I engaged him in conversation and learned that he was a Dr. Treadway. When he told me that he had taken his medical course at the University of Virginia in the first class graduated after the Civil War, I recalled that my father had also been a member of that class. "Do you remember a classmate by the name of Brooks," I asked? "Certainly I do—Zachary Taylor Brooks,"—and at once, as I had heard my father do, he called verbatim the names of the entire class. He was a typical old-school country doctor, whose mission in life was to relieve mankind of its misery but not to relieve it of its money.

Impressed by the country, I confided to him that in earlier years I had dreamed of marrying a Shenandoah Valley maid and spending my life on one of its beautiful farms.

"No," said he, "the last is all right but socially it does not compare with the people of Eastern Virginia. Most of this section was settled after the Revolution by left-over Hessians and they are not our kind of people." With a wife and two babies, this dissolution of a boyish dream left me prepared to move on.

We stopped over to visit the Gettysburg battlefield, where so many gallant Carolina boys lay buried—lost in their fruitless efforts to take Cemetery Ridge. A few years later I revisited the scene as a commissioner appointed to dedicate a statue designed by Gutzon Borglum to commemorate Carolina's troops who fell during Pickett's famous charge.

My stay at Bay Head was interrupted by an urgent telephone message calling me home to defend Dr. Taylor, a prominent oculist of Greensboro, who had been arrested along with his secretary and charged with fornication and adultery. Upon my return I found that a preliminary trial had already been held before the City judge and they were bound over to the Superior Court for an early trial. In conferences both vehemently denied their guilt, and Dr. Taylor asserted that the warrant had been sworn out by his wife on account of a family row. Upon further inquiry I learned that the wife and their only daughter, a bright sixteen-year-old girl, had both testified unequivocally to a shameful cohabitation between the doctor and his secretary in their home over a period of twelve months. Dr. Taylor's explanation was that his co-defendant, a country girl, had come to him for treatment of her eyes, which were badly crossed, impairing her vision; that he had corrected the trouble, but that she had little money with which to pay and she was given employment in his office as an assistant to work it out and had become very efficient; that she had met his wife, and he took her to his home to live.

The wife, who had independent means, had employed Judges Bynum and Strickland to assist the solicitor in the prosecution, which meant a fight to the finish. Searching for a possible defense I suggested to the secretary that she have a physical examination to show that the hymen had not been ruptured, as she earnestly asserted that she had never had sexual intercourse with anyone. To my surprise she demurred, without giving any particular reason.

The next day she called at my office and opened the interview by saying that her reason for dreading the examination was that it would disclose that her hymen had been ruptured. This was the last straw, and I saw visions of a prompt conviction and a severe sentence awaiting the trial. She must have noticed my expression of despair and even doubt of her innocence, for she calmly drew from her handbag a paper writing and handed it to me. I was never more surprised and shocked than I was when I saw staring me in the face a message from my lately deceased father in his own handwriting, completely answering why an examination of this poor girl was not necessary. It came like a message from the grave. In substance it was as follows:

To Whom It May Concern:
On the night of February 1, 1920, I was called to give professional care to Miss ——, who had sustained an internal injury from a fall in the bathtub. In treating her I found it necessary to make an exploratory examination of her vagina and organs. In doing so it became necessary for me to rupture the hymen which I found intact.

I am giving her this statement as a precaution if she should ever need it.

Z. T. Brooks, M. D.

The supreme value of this declaration if I could get it in evidence was that it bore a date months after the wife and daughter had already sworn that the accused began their illegal intercourse. I realized that I had in possession an atomic bomb for this case; but I was faced with one legal difficulty and a serious personal embarrassment. The legal difficulty was to make the paper writing competent, since it was not made under oath and its author was dead. My personal embarrassment arose from the fact that the writer was my deceased father, the document was unusual, and even its authenticity might be questioned.

The trial attracted much attention, and the courthouse

crowd reveled in the testimony of the wife and the daughter, which described in detail how, twelve months before, the doctor had established his secretary in one of the best rooms in the house, had lain in bed with her night after night, and had entirely abandoned his wife's bed; that they had become so bold and abandoned that on Sunday mornings he required sometimes his wife and sometimes the daughter to serve them breakfast in bed. On cross-examination they never faltered or wavered in the testimony disclosing as sordid a story of infidelity and lewdness as was ever listened to.

I took particular pains to fix the beginning of the *corpus delicti* several months before February 1, the date named in my father's declaration, which was in my pocket, but its existence was totally unknown to counsel for the State. Dr. Taylor and his secretary testified to their innocence and denied all the charges of the prosecution, but the tide was running high against them. I still held my ace trump in my pocket, and before offering it in evidence I called as witnesses doctors, lawyers, bankers, and druggists, by whom I proved the genuineness of the paper writing and signature of my father. When it was offered in evidence, a storm of objections arose from all the lawyers for the prosecution, who insisted that it was incompetent, misleading, and irrelevant.

James Webb, the presiding judge, an able and experienced officer, asked to see the paper and carefully read it over. Turning to counsel for the State he said: "Gentlemen, the genuineness of this paper writing cannot be and is not questioned. You may be correct in arguing that technically it is not admissible as evidence. I am disposed to think it is, but be that as it may, if I exclude it and the jury should convict, I shall not hesitate to set the verdict aside. Justice demands that the defendants have the benefit of this very material matter before reaching a verdict." It was read to the jury and a verdict of not guilty followed.

After the trial I pressed the doctor for a reason why his wife and daughter conspired against him with such viciousness. His explanation was that he objected to his daughter's having secret dates with questionable boys and to stop it he finally laid her across his knees and spanked her, for which neither she nor her mother ever forgave him and thereafter vented their spleen upon him.

Perhaps the only moral to be drawn from this sordid and immoral affair is that a father should never spank a sixteen-year-old daughter because she loves not wisely, but too well.

One day a prominent business man, very much excited, came into my office with a copy of a complaint which had just been served on him, in which $10,000 damages was sought by a husband for an attempted intimacy with his wife. These charges he emphatically denied and gave me the following astonishing story:

The defendant had employed the plaintiff as a cigar salesman in Charlotte, North Carolina, and he had come to Greensboro for a conference with the defendant. He had phoned one morning that he and his wife were in an apartment in Greensboro but that he was not well enough to go to see the defendant and asked if he would come to his apartment—giving the defendant his address. The defendant went, and after discussing business for a few minutes the plaintiff asked to be excused so that he might go to a drugstore to get some medicine. This left the defendant and the plaintiff's wife alone in the room. She was a striking-looking young blonde. Shortly after her husband left she excused herself from the room and in a few minutes returned with nothing on but a kimono, took a seat on the defendant's lap, and began fondling him. He became suspicious, but humored her along until he could graciously leave. Soon the husband walked in on them in this position and raised Cain.

The defendant, a prominent hotel man and manufacturer of cigars, upon receiving the complaint, suddenly realized and feared the publicity of it all. I told him that it looked like a badger game and that the thing to do was to get time to answer, employ a detective, and find out about the history of this man and his wife.

He engaged a detective who immediately went to work on the case. In about ten days the defendant came up to me with a smile and said, "We have the dead wood on them." The detective had learned that the couple had moved to Charlotte from Norfolk; so he went to Norfolk and there found that they were never married; that the husband had a living wife from whom he had never been divorced; and that the woman had come to Norfolk from Baltimore. This, of course, put an end to the case as there could be no damage if the man and woman were not married. However, the detective, not content with what he had already learned, went on to Baltimore and found that the woman had a record there also. She had had an affair in Baltimore with the son of the governor and had tried to blackmail him. The story of that affair was written up in all of the Baltimore papers and the *Baltimore Sun* carried her picture on the front page. When I filed the answer I told the whole story, and attached a copy of the paper with her picture. The day after the answer was filed, the man and his woman left town, and Judges Bynum and Strudwick, who represented them, were left high and dry without clients.

22

The Cole Case

PERHAPS because of my ten years' service as prosecuting attorney, I was occasionally employed in the trial of criminal cases. One of the most important and sensational was for the defense in *State* v. *Cole,* at Rockingham, North Carolina, in the eastern part of the state.

W. B. Cole, a millionaire manufacturer, was indicted for shooting and killing young Bill Ormond, the son of a prominent Methodist minister, who was a suitor of Cole's only daughter. The trial was so celebrated that a drama was written about it called "Coquette," in which Helen Hayes played the leading role during a long run on Broadway.

A battery of fifteen of the state's ablest trial lawyers was engaged on either side. My associates selected me to take the lead in arguing the law to the presiding judge (Findley), examining and cross-examining most of the witnesses, and making the closing argument to the jury. It was one of the toughest and most taxing trials of my life. On account of the prominence of the principals, the attributes of love, jealousy, revenge, and tragedy involved, the trial day after day brought to the spacious courtroom men and women from all parts of the state until standing room was at a premium. The defendant, because of the aggravated circumstances of the killing, was denied bond and committed to jail to await trial. Local feeling was so intense that, at the request of the State, the judge impaneled a jury from another county.

The State's evidence showed that the deceased, a returned veteran of World War I, drove his car in midday to the front of the defendant's office on Main Street, and was sitting there when the defendant came out of his office with pistol in hand, walked to the car, and shot the deceased, killing him instantly. Under North Carolina law this was seemingly first degree murder.

The facts relied upon for the defense were that the defendant's only daughter, to whom he was deeply attached, had become engaged to the deceased, and the father, learning of it, had advised her not to marry him because he was thriftless, irresponsible, and unworthy of her. The daughter had told the deceased of her father's objections to him, and had said that her affection and regard for her father were such that she would not marry him without her father's consent. This infuriated the young man, who more than once threatened to kill Mr. Cole, to whom these threats were communicated.

Determined not to be thwarted, Bill Ormond finally wrote Mr. Cole a letter, stating that he and Cole's daughter were in love and that they had been living together as man and wife for a year. He urged the father to consent to their marriage. Upon receipt of this letter, Mr. Cole took his daughter for a horseback ride in the country and showed her the letter. He asked her if the statement of their intimacy was true. She assured him that it was false and that under no circumstances would she think of marrying Ormond. When the deceased learned of her decision he became reckless and showed to his pals around town copies of the letter he had written to Mr. Cole. He also annoyed the defendant by repeatedly driving back and forth before the Cole home, honking his automobile horn.

Under the strain and humiliation, Mr. Cole's health broke; he lost his appetite and weight, lost control of his organs, and could not sleep; and finally his nervous and mental condition became impaired. He employed counsel to try and persuade the deceased to let him and his family alone. When this failed, fearing for his life, he put a pistol in the drawer of his office desk. When the deceased, on the day of the homicide, parked his car in front of the defendant's office, Cole thought Ormond had come to make good his threats to kill him and, in desperation he fired upon the young man.

Rockingham was a small town and feeling was intense. Some thought Cole guilty; others, not guilty. Eastern North Carolina became aroused and divided over the case. The American Legion employed counsel to prosecute. The lawyers on either side fought every step of the way and the trial lasted for three weeks.

One of the highlights of the trial came when we offered the daughter as a witness for her father. Counsel for the state had intimated that if she were put upon the witness stand they would cross-examine her about numerous letters which she had written the deceased; that these were very damaging to her character; and that they had these letters in their possession. As she took the witness chair one of the State's counsel arose and said, "If this witness is allowed to testify, then all of these letters become competent evidence against her." I replied, "Your Honor, we offer before this court as a witness a perfect virgin; let the State do its worst!" She was examined and cross-examined, but no letters were ever offered to impugn her.

During the long trial another interesting circumstance occurred. It was brought to our attention that the deceased had a pistol lying beside him on the seat of his automobile when he was shot. We set about to check the fact and found that a friend had driven the car, immediately after the shooting, to a garage, and had concealed the pistol. A young lady in town who was at the garage had seen the pistol but did not know what had become of it. We finally got possession of it, and it was a very important factor. But how could we prove that the deceased had possessed the pistol and that this was the same pistol?

We finally decided to bring the pistol into court and lay it on our table in view of the jury. We then asked a witness for the State if this was the pistol found lying on the seat beside the deceased. A roar of opposition came from the State saying that there was no evidence that the deceased had a pistol. We replied that the question was an innocent one if the witness had not seen the pistol. The witness knew nothing about the pistol and said so, as we knew he would. Each succeeding witness was asked the same question and each gave a negative reply. By this time the jury became interested in the pistol, which was kept prominently displayed, and after about two days of this, the State, knowing that the deceased did have a pistol and that we had posesssion of it, decided that the jury might think the State guilty of suppressing testimony. Under this pressure, the State said, "We admit that the deceased had a pistol at his side when shot."

I shall never forget the closing hours of this historic trial. The jury had been given the case Saturday afternoon. On Sunday morning, the third week of the trial, just as the church bells were tolling for services, the sheriff notified counsel that the jury was ready to render its verdict.

We gathered in the court room, Cole was brought in from the jail where he had been confined and sat down at the lawyers' table. Sensing his counsel's suspense, he calmly said, "I'm not afraid. I am prepared for the result." The jurors filed in and took their accustomed seats in the jury box. "Have you agreed upon your verdict, gentlemen?" asked the clerk of the court. They in unison replied, "We have." Cole was directed to stand up, and the clerk inquired, "Mr. Foreman, do you find the prisoner at the bar, W. B. Cole, guilty or not guilty as charged in the bill of indictment?" Breaking a deathly silence, the foreman arose and in solemn tones answered, "We find him not guilty."

23

Retribution in History

THERE is an old saying among newspaper men that for a dog to bite a man is no news, but for a man to bite a dog is news. Similarly, it is no news for North Carolina to go Democratic, but it was news for Hoover to defeat Al Smith for the presidency in 1928 by more than 50,000 majority.

I attended the National Democratic Convention in New York in 1924, when Smith and McAdoo struggled unsuccessfully for a week to secure the nomination for president. I did not support McAdoo because I felt the party had already honored him beyond his deserts; I did not support Smith because I felt sure he could not be elected. I supported John W. Davis, with whom I had been associated in important litigation, whom I regarded as the better equipped for the place on account of his background, learning, and culture, and who was universally regarded as among the greatest legal debaters at the American bar. It was at this convention that Franklin D. Roosevelt, in nominating Smith, called him "The Happy Warrior."

By 1928 Smith had so gained in popular favor among the

Democratic leaders of the nation that his nomination was foreshadowed. I felt that he had earned the nomination, but I still believed that he could not be elected, not because he was wet but because he was a Catholic.

There was more political hypocrisy manifested in this campaign between Smith and Hoover than I have ever known before or since. The North Carolina vote is a perfect illustration. The people of the state knew little of and cared less for Hoover; they personally admired Al Smith and his "Sidewalks of New York"; and of the voting prohibitionists, too many liked liquor as well as Smith to quit their party and vote for a Republican president on that account alone. Whiskey was the excuse which many saintly ones made, but the real reason was Catholicism. The contest was in what Mencken called the Bible Belt, and that Bible was a Protestant Bible as expounded by the three Johns and not by the Pope from St. Peter's in Rome.

Simmons sensed the political danger and induced Cordell Hull to enter his name as presidential candidate in the state primary. I purposely refrained from taking an active part in the primary, which, as the contest grew, left me on the side lines. As the time for the state convention approached, nearly everybody was fighting mad and the people were pretty evenly divided. In the face of this situation Governor Angus W. McLean and Attorney General Dennis G. Brummitt, who was state chairman, called me to Raleigh with the request that I make the keynote address and preside over the convention. They expressed deep concern over party harmony and, by having a chairman who was not a partisan on either side, hoped to keep the convention from breaking up in a row. It was a tough assignment and I accepted it as a duty. Never shall I forget the sea of serious faces that filled the auditorium to overflowing as I stood on the platform. There were no histrionics, no mirth, no horseplay. The tenseness was so great that you could almost cut it with a knife, and some of the delegates looked as if they might have knives in their pockets.

Conscious that the angry convention might not let anyone speak, I opened my address in as light a vein as I knew how: "As Paul said to the jailer, 'Do yourself no harm, we are all here.'" This seemed to amuse them. They allowed me to finish my address, which was purposely not controversial, but from then on the delegates howled down every speaker, including Clyde R. Hoey and Cameron Morrison. The delegates had met for action and not oratory and, as future events showed, this was the beginning of a fight that was to result in putting the state in the national Republican column and the powerful Senator Simmons out of office.

Simmons was a delegate to the national convention that nominated Smith, but when John J. Raskob was made national chairman, Simmons seized upon this as an excuse to bolt the party nominee and joined with Frank McNinch in a crusade against Smith's election. No greater political surprise has ever occurred in the state. For twenty-eight years Simmons had been in the Senate and the political boss of the state. He tolerated no party disloyalty and applied the whip even to moderate dissenters. His apostasy has never been fully explained or accounted for; yet with courage and abandon he marched through a bloody slaughter-house to his political grave. Many of his old associates turned on him, and the party workers down to the voting precincts took up the cry, "Away with him."

Ex-Governor Angus W. McLean was his natural successor from every point of view, when two years later Simmons came up for re-election. McLean was urged to make the race, but he declined, stating that he and Simmons had been life-long friends and party intimates; that Simmons had rendered a great service to the state and was now an old and infirm man; and that because he had made one serious blunder for conscience's sake he would not turn on him and drive him in humiliation from the United States Senate. But no such scruples animated Josiah W. Bailey, whom Simmons had made politically. He turned on Simmons as if he were a stranger and relentlessly pursued him, rallying to his own support not only his former friends but also the old political enemies which he and the Senator had fought hand in hand for a quarter of a century. Bailey was elected, but democracy has not been the better served. They both at heart were Hamiltonians and neither ever believed in the "New Freedom," the "Square Deal," or the "New Deal." Their idol was the God of the *status quo*.

Angus W. McLean and I had been friends from our college days at the University of North Carolina. When he announced his candidacy for the governorship, J. W. Bailey opposed him in a vigorous campaign. One of the serious charges made against him was that while acting as assistant treasurer of the United States he had approved a policy of the secretary of Agriculture which resulted in greatly reducing the price of agricultural products. At McLean's request I was selected to prepare his defense. I went to Washington and after consultation with government officials and senators, I wrote his reply, which was carried in the press throughout the state and one hundred thousand copies were printed and circulated.

United States Senator Lee S. Overman, who had long served the state as an acceptable senator, was growing old and feeble and it was thought that McLean would appoint his successor. It was understood that he had me in mind for the position, but Senator Overman lingered on until Governor O. Max Gardner's administration and he gave the appointment to former Governor Cameron Morrison.

24

Roosevelt and the New Deal

THE year 1932 was a busy one for me in business, politics, and law. In the early part of the year, as previously mentioned, I broke with the management of the Jefferson Standard Life Insurance Company, dissolved my firm, and established a new firm under the name of Brooks, Parker & Holderness, with offices in the Southeastern Building. Later, during the spring, I was employed in the Cannon-Reynolds-Holman case, which was destined to engage my legal services for several years.

The year before, for the graduation exercises at the Woman's College in Greensboro (now a part of the University of North Carolina), Mrs. Eleanor Roosevelt had been invited to deliver an address. The college authorities requested that we entertain Mrs. Roosevelt in our home, which we did, and she spent several days in and around Greensboro making speeches before various groups. Before leaving she said to me that she would be glad for her husband, Franklin, to know me, and asked if I would be available to go to Warm Springs, Georgia, where he was taking treatment, to see him. I told her that I would be, and some weeks later I received a telegram from Mr. Roosevelt inviting me down.

I spent two days with him and had a very enlightening experience. He discussed with me the general outlines of his campaign for the presidency, and particularly emphasized his desire to have a Supreme Court which was in sympathy with the objects he had in mind. He remarked that he saw no objection to an *entente cordiale* between the Chief Executive and members of the Supreme Court such as had existed at Albany during his administration as governor of New York. He said that the judges could be of great assistance to the Chief Executive by advising with him from time to time as to the constitutionality of certain measures which he wished to see passed, not committing them to a decision of any particular case but discussing with them the general outline of his proposals. I assured him that I would be glad to support him for the presidency and would use my influence to this end in North Carolina.

It was about this time that a vacancy occurred on the Supreme Court of the United States, and as the Fourth Circuit, which comprised the states of Maryland, Virginia, West Virginia, North Carolina, and South Carolina, had not had an appointee on the bench since the Civil War, there was an insistent demand that an appointment from this circuit be made. My friends throughout the state, including former Governor Angus W. McLean, United States District Judge Johnson J. Hayes, E. T. Cansler of Charlotte, Tam Bowie of Jefferson, and many other leaders of the bar wrote and wired to President Hoover and Attorney General Henry L. Stimson recommending me for the appointment. I had occasion to visit Mr. Roosevelt again while in Philadelphia that year, and he discussed with me the appointment to the Supreme Court. He remarked that when he saw that a vacancy had occurred he had thought of me in connection with it and that if a situation arose in which the President was disposed to go South for his appointment he would be glad to communicate with Senator Wagner of New York and ask him to urge my appointment. President Hoover, however, gave the appointment to Judge Benjamin N. Cardozo of the Court of Appeals in New York, which was a better appointment.

From the early spring of 1932 until his nomination, I received numerous letters from Mr. Roosevelt. In April I wrote him as follows:

April 2, 1932

Dear Governor Roosevelt:

Governor Gardner invited Angus McLean, Josephus Daniels, and me for luncheon yesterday at the Mansion, to confer with Mr. Homer Cummings about your affairs in this State. I assume that Mr. Cummings will give you a detailed report of the meeting.

After a considerable discussion, it was agreed that in view of the fact that your candidacy was receiving such universal support from the people, it was probably best, for the present, not to have any formal organization.

Under our system, the Congressional Districts elect two delegates and two alternates, and the State Convention usually sends four delegates at large. The State Convention has authority to instruct the delegates at large, but does not have the authority to instruct the District delegates. The word will be passed around to your friends in the various Districts to seek to have these delegates instructed by the District Conventions.

The unanimous opinion was expressed yesterday, and I think this is in keeping with the facts, that you will get the entire delegation from North Carolina. The only possible obstacle is the attitude of the Duke Power interests and the Carolina Light and Power Company. As I explained to you at Warm Springs, these interests exert a dominating influence over the only people, except the tobacco companies, that have any free money left, and, as you know, they don't hesitate to use it to influence political results. I also expressed the opinion to you that these gentlemen would not come out in the open if they found that the people were insisting upon your nomination. This is precisely what has happened. It is really very touching to observe the admiration that some of these new converts to your cause are exhibiting. Frankly, the only danger I see to your supporters in North Carolina is that in the grand rush to get on the band-wagon, some of them may get hurt.

It is gratifying to observe the very remarkable support which the people are according your candidacy in every section of the country. The Smith fiasco has definitely helped you in this section, and, I think, almost everywhere. Current political and economic events are also contributing largely to your cause. The day of the glorification of Big Business and the rich, merely on account of their possessions and power, it seems to me, has definitely passed. On the other hand, your attitude in meeting and dealing with public questions is increasingly impressing the public with the fact that you know what it is all about, and are determined to meet and deal with them in the spirit of enlightened liberalism.

When at Warm Springs, you remarked to me that you were considering coming down by automobile through the Shenandoah Valley on your spring visit to Georgia. If I may be permitted to speak of war to Napoleon, would it not be well to stop at Lexington, Virginia, and observe the very beautiful recumbent statue of General Robert E. Lee? Theodore Roosevelt said of him, in his life of Thomas H. Benton, that Lee was one of the greatest generals that the English speaking race had ever produced. I think the almost universal opinion, both in the North and South, now is that the two great figures emerging from the Civil War period were Lincoln and Lee. Lincoln's Gettysburg speech and Lee's memorial might serve as a worthwhile connecting thought in some future oration that you may make.

I am arranging to encourage the organization of the Roosevelt-for-President Club in Greensboro, and especially for the reason that one of the leading daily papers of the State is published here, the Greensboro Daily News, and the doings of this club and its advocacy of an instructed delegation by the Districts of the State will receive statewide publicity, and thus call the matter to the attention of your friends throughout the State.

Very sincerely,

A. L. Brooks

Governor Franklin D. Roosevelt
Executive Mansion
Albany, New York

To this letter I received the following reply:

April 28th, 1932

Hon. A. L. Brooks,
1009-1017 Jefferson Standard Bldg.,
Greensboro, N. C.

My dear Judge:—

Although I shall soon be in Warm Springs at which time I hope to have the pleasure of talking things over with you, I want to acknowledge your recent letter with its report on the progress of affairs in North Carolina. I need not tell you how much I appreciate the personal time and thought which you have devoted on my behalf, nor need I assure you that your judgment is one in which I have great confidence.

I have heard from other friends of the activity of the club in Greensboro, and the friendly support of the local paper. Although I have made few detailed plans for my weeks in Georgia, I have not forgotten your suggestion that I motor through the Shenandoah Valley either going or coming.

With cordial personal regards,
Yours very sincerely,
FRANKLIN D. ROOSEVELT

On May 7, reporting on the progress of his campaign in North Carolina, I wrote Mr. Roosevelt:

With respect to North Carolina, the delegation will undoubtedly be very largely—perhaps unanimously—for you. Still, I find that there is a disposition among some of our leaders in high place not to instruct the delegates. I believe an instruction could be easily carried, but it may become a question as to whether it is wise to press it. The masses in North Carolina are overwhelmingly for you, but the power interests, while not active, are urging through their friends, most of whom I think you have a line on, an uninstructed delegation. Speaking generally, the situation here is not materially unlike the Alabama situation, and with the same producing causes.

To this Mr. Roosevelt replied from Warm Springs on May 9:

...I very distinctly and definitely hope that the North Carolina delegation will actually be instructed for me—for the very good reason that the Shouse crowd have been talking uninstructed delegations and even where the delegation is friendly to me, but uninstructed, this same crowd claims an immediate and far-reaching victory. I hope that you will do everything possible to get instructions.

On June 16 I wired Mr. Roosevelt from Raleigh that the delegates from North Carolina had been instructed for him, and followed it by a letter in which I said:

At a county convention here I offered a resolution, copy of which I have sent you, instructing for you. To my surprise, Senator Bailey's political manager, Mr. C. L. Shuping, who lives here, opposed these instructions, claiming that he was your manager in the state. Just how he got to be, I don't know. Mr. Daniels, learning of it, phoned me that he did not understand the situation at all, and advised that I should come to Raleigh at once, which I did. He and I got busy then with the delegates as they came in, and I found that the powers-that-be were seeking to let the matter ease by without any general instructions, saying that this was the usual policy in this state. Mr. Daniels and I both forced the issue, declaring that it was your desire that instructions should be had. The happy result you were apprised of.

On the 17th I received the following telegram from Mr. Roosevelt:

Albany NY via Raleigh NCar 17 137p

Aubrey L. Brooks
Greensboro, NCar

I am made very happy by North Carolina action My deep thanks for all that you have done for me.

FRANKLIN D. ROOSEVELT

After Mr. Roosevelt's election I entertained the hope that I might receive an appointment to the United States Supreme

Court bench, but no vacancy occurred until 1937, when Justice Hugo Black was appointed. I made no effort to secure the appointment because by that time I was sixty-six years old—beyond the period when justices of the Supreme Court of the United States were thought to be eligible. My legal engagements, also, had become so numerous and exacting that my duty to clients, and financial considerations as well, left me in no position to accept an appointment under the administration.

This state of affairs continued throughout Mr. Roosevelt's occupancy of the White House. However, my zeal for his continued success and re-elections never abated. I took part in all the succeeding campaigns by making speeches, contributing to campaign expenses, and otherwise advocating Mr. Roosevelt's continuance in office. His New Deal program in the main I felt was at last a fulfillment of the hopes and aspirations of the plain people of America. His farm program alone would entitle him to immortality. The neglected farmer had struggled amid poverty and want, but now he was assured of a decent living and an opportunity to educate his children. This phase of Roosevelt's program was particularly appealing to me because I was reared on a farm and knew the hardships resulting from seven dollars a hundred for tobacco and forty cents a bushel for wheat and corn.

Roosevelt curbed the gamblers of Wall Street by the enactment of the Securities Act of 1933 and the Securities Exchange Act of 1934; he opened the banks of the country and gave confidence to depositors that their accounts were safe; and last but not least he instituted a program of home building for the underprivileged. The thousands of homes now dotting the landscape throughout the nation are a living testimonial to his devotion to the welfare of Abraham Lincoln's common man.

25

Pleasure and Profit of Travel

A CERTAIN amount of leisure is a prerequisite to enjoyable travel, but extended absence from an active law practice is always a problem. The only solution I have found is to associate capable younger partners who can carry on in one's absence.

My wife and I enjoy travel and through the years we have indulged this pleasure. Our first journey in such contentment was a 250-miles horseback ride through the Blue Ridge Mountains in the summer of 1917. That year the North Carolina Bar Association, of which I was president, met in Asheville. To get there I shipped our saddle horses to Wilkesboro, and for ten days we leisurely rode along unpaved country roads lined with gorgeous rhododendron and azaleas. With only a haversack attached to the saddles, we sometimes spent the nights in farmhouses along the way, wherever night overtook us. We passed through Jefferson, Boone, Blowing Rock, and Linville. One of our most engaging stops for a night was at a farmhouse beyond Bakersville, located on the upper branch of New River. When the housewife called us for supper we were greeted at the table by the sight of a large vegetable dish loaded with broiled rainbow trout. The fact that they had been caught with a seine offended my Izaak Walton sensibilities, but did not mar the pleasure of eating them.

Since I had never visited Europe, my wife encouraged me in 1921 to join a lifelong friend, Dr. John Williams, in a trip abroad, while she kept the home fires burning and two restless young boys out of devilment.

For three months we traveled over Europe, saw staid England and its cathedrals, gay Paris and the Louvre, the battlefields of France and the poppy fields of Flanders. We visited Germany, rode to Munich along the River Rhine, which had so recently run red with the blood of our boys, visited Oberammergau and witnessed the Passion Play depicting the crucifixion of Christ. Thence we went to the beautiful city of Vienna, lying prostrate from the ravages of war; to Florence, made famous by the Medici during the Renaissance; to lovely Venice, perpetual playground of romance; to Rome, once the capital of a world empire and the author of a timeless jurisprudence—a city where Michelangelo and Leonardo da Vinci worked, where past history was memorialized by its ruins and the future was symbolized by St. Peter's, the center of a world-wide religion.

Finally we traveled along the shores of the Adriatic to Milan, whose grand cathedral represents man's loftiest expression in architectural beauty dedicated to the glory of God.

Upon returning to England, I was invited, through the grace of a letter from John W. Davis, late Ambassador, to lunch with an English chancellor, and later sat with him upon the woolsack and observed the prompt administration of English justice.

Two years later my wife and I took a Mediterranean cruise. Its unalloyed pleasure still lingers in memory's storehouse, as we recall the visit to the cradle of civilization and the founding of man's hope and belief in the immortality of the soul.

Never-to-be-forgotten was my first view of Athens. A stroll through the ruins of this city, once goddess of them all, filled one with horror at the wantonness of man. But looming above it stood the matchless Acropolis. In Athens, yielding to recollections of things past, we could almost feel the presence of many of the world's immortals who from time to time had passed through its portals: Here Homer may have sung; Socrates, Plato, and Aristotle expounded their philosophies; Euripides and Aristophanes enthralled the multitudes with their immortal dramas; and St. Paul first preached the saving grace of Christianity.

Continuing our voyage we next passed through the Bosporus Straits and visited Constantinople, the city made famous as the seat of the Roman Empire and by its founder's having adopted the Christian religion and made the city a Christian stronghold, which enabled it to withstand the barbarian hordes for a thousand years, because, as the historian Gibbon says, "The Christians outlived, out-fought, and out-died them."

Thence we went to Palestine and Jerusalem, where sacred history was written and the Christian religion was born; to Cairo, the crossroads of the East, where we saw the awe-inspiring pyramids and the inscrutable sphynx. We viewed the body of Ramses II in its mausoleum preserved through thousands of years substantially unchanged; and traveled up the Nile River for five hundred miles to see the tomb of Tut-ankh-amen, whose elaborate arrangements showed that the domestic problems of the future life had been taken care of. Returning, we saw the sapphire-like bay of Naples, revisited Rome, and heard of its budding new hero and Romeo, Benito Mussolini.

For some years we interspersed our summers by visits to Canada and a trip to Alaska, which this country fortunately acquired from Russia when a relationship existed that made sense, and thus incidentally gained for ourselves a highly prized buffer territory against Communism.

A wag in Greensboro has a saying already quoted that this or that man "made the wrong mistake." I was that man in 1929 when, extended in the stock market on margins, I left for Scotland to shoot grouse with my friends, the Brights of New York, who had taken a large lease near Balmoral Castle, the summer home of the King. It was the grand experience of a lifetime, but my host and I came back to face a financial debacle that shook us all. Between my own and clients' troubles, our pleasure trips were limited to short cruises to the West Indies and Panama Canal, and one summer in Mexico City and its environs.

For a long while I had wanted to visit Russia and observe the conditions existing in a country that had undergone so violent a political, social, and economic revolution. An opportunity came in 1936, and we took passage from New York with a party of friends on a Scandinavian-Russian cruise. When we reached Leningrad, I realized that we were in the presence of history—some sacred, but mostly profane. A visit to the Imperial Palace revealed an amazing collection of rare paintings, portraits, and other objects of art and beauty. Here too was shown the bedchamber of Catherine the Great, with its accommodating bed facing an elevated garden through which her frequent lovers were conducted in hopeless effort to satisfy her insatiable passion. The Czars had founded a great empire, ruled and enjoyed by its nobility, but now the Bolshevists were in charge, and the ruthless master, Stalin, firmly seated in the Kremlin, held in the palm of his hand the destiny of Russia's millions of helpless souls. Evidence of the results of his five-year program were to be seen. Everybody, men and women alike, had been put to work; the nobles had been liquidated and many kulaks as well. Most of the many churches in Moscow had been razed and their sites developed into parks and playgrounds for the proletariat. The cobblestone streets were supplanted by well-laid concrete, and a three-hundred-mile spacious hard-surface road had been built connecting Leningrad and Moscow. The printing press was busy, and universal education was encouraged. The subway stations of Moscow were finished in ornate marble and made the subways of New York look like back alleys. But the universal appearance of the people was one of want, reflecting an unhappy past and an uncertain future.

To me, the crowning experience came when I was taken to the hill overlooking Moscow and shown where Napoleon sat on his white charger and saw the city go down in flames and his dream of world empire go up in smoke. The very thought of it kindled remembrance of his gallant charge across the bridge at Lodi, his masterful triumphs upon the battlefields of Austerlitz and Marengo. Not until the Russian campaign was his famous guard ever defeated. The sublimity and the sadness of it all recalled Gray's famous line, "The paths of glory lead but to the grave."

From Russia to the Scandinavian countries, where we next visited, is geographically a long way, but ideologically the two countries are even farther apart. The one has established a communistic system of government without God, while the other has adopted a democracy under God. Norway, Sweden, and Denmark, even with their kings, have demonstrated that man is capable of self-government without tyranny, with freedom to enjoy life, liberty, and the pursuit of happiness. Their natural resources, state-owned or controlled, are employed to serve the public and not for the enrichment of the few.

The last leg of this cruise landed us in Edinburgh, that ancient Scottish city of learning, culture, and Protestantism, the home of John Knox and Sir Walter Scott. From there we motored through England's beautiful and peaceful lake country to London, and bade farewell to a continent so soon to be drenched with the blood of a second world war.

Our last "journey in contentment" took us to the Hawaiian Islands in February before the Japs struck in December. Honolulu, the gateway and gem of the Pacific, has all the virtues of the tropical Orient with the comforts and conveniences of the Occident added. A month spent among the interesting islands with headquarters at the Royal Hawaiian Hotel facing Waikiki's glorious beach, enveloped with flowers, charmed with sweet music, and entertained by hula-hula dancing, made one ask, "Why ever leave?"

From the soft and balmy waves of the Pacific, en route home we visited the cold, snow-covered mountains of Yosemite National Park. A drive through this Park in midwinter can never be forgotten. But with all its beauty, the most impressive sight is the great redwood trees towering heavenward, standing through many centuries, a silent reminder that we are still babes in the woods.

26

The Cannon-Reynolds-Holman Case

THE combination of marriages which mismated millions of dollars, and suspected murder, made the Cannon-Reynolds-Holman case of great public concern, and the newspapers of the nation carried screaming headlines about it. Beginning with the mistakes of two spoiled, rich minors, it ran its dramatic course for eight years through the state courts, and the final chapter was written by the Supreme Court of the United States.

Zachary Smith Reynolds, a son of R. J. Reynolds, founder of the Reynolds Tobacco Company, in 1930 married Anne Cannon, the lovely daughter of Joe Cannon, a son of J. W. Cannon, who was founder of the Cannon Mills. Unfortunately, the couple were too young and immature to undertake the responsibilities of a home and family. In less than a year they parted, Smith Reynolds going to Europe and leaving his pregnant wife to endure her troubles alone.

Failure of the families to effect a reconciliation resulted in my employment by Anne's father to secure a separation agreement and suitable provision for her and the child's support and education. W. N. Reynolds, the uncle of Smith and his guardian, was most co-operative in working out a settlement satisfactory to the parties and to both families. An agreement was reached, subject to the approval of the courts, by which the wife was to receive for life the income from a trust fund of $500,000, the principal at her death to go to her child; the daughter was to receive outright $500,000 to be held in trust for her benefit until she reached maturity. After a full hearing, the court approved the settlement.

Some months later Anne went to Reno and there secured a divorce. Within a few days after the decree was entered, Smith married Libby Holman, a "torch singer" on Broadway.

A deplorable state of affairs had seemingly been settled to the satisfaction of everyone concerned, but the fates were soon to decree differently. The state was shocked one morning to learn from the Associated Press that Smith Reynolds had been shot to death the night before at his ancestral home "Reynolda," where he and his wife were staying. Deep secrecy surrounded the tragedy, but the finger of guilt pointed to his wife, who was arrested and charged with murder. Because of the lack of any direct positive evidence and the wish of the family to avoid the notoriety and scandal of a trial, the prosecution was dropped and she was released.

The known facts, when pieced together, tended to show that on the night of the homicide Libby Holman had as her guest Blanche Yurka, an actress from New York, and a few other friends. They were making free use of the swimming pool and all were drinking. Smith Reynolds and his wife Libby had been quarreling during the day and he had packed his grip, telling her that he was through with her. He left the home, saying he was going into Winston-Salem to spend the night. He apparently was the only sober one in the crowd. Some hours later, he unexpectedly returned, and later was found lying across a dishevelled bed with a bullet through his head. All evidence showed that he had been killed.

Libby Holman, Blanche Yurka, and Ab Walker, who was Smith Reynolds' secretary, were the only ones who had access to the room and each denied the killing. Ab Walker, a young man in his early twenties, said that he knew how Smith had been killed, but neither then nor since has he told. Libby Holman, who was in a maudlin condition, denied any knowledge of the shooting. Strangest of all, when the authorities arrived, there was no pistol to be found, but later one was found in plain view lying on the floor of the room in which Smith was shot. It had evidently in the meantime been placed there by someone.

Zachary Smith Reynolds' death left a Pandora's box of legal problems about what was to become of his huge fortune. The legal eye will at once see looming the serious question of the validity of the first wife's divorce, the legality of the second marriage of Smith, and consequently the legitimacy of the Holman baby, born after Smith Reynolds' murder. A further complication existed because Smith had attempted, before marrying Libby Holman, to make a will excluding his first wife and daughter. Smith was a minor, and made the will in New York State, where it was lawful to make such a will; but under the laws of North Carolina a minor could not make a valid will. Since, therefore, he had died intestate, Anne Cannon Reynolds, 2nd, remained his only legitimate heir.

Confronted with this involved and complicated situation, W. N. Reynolds, head of the Reynolds Tobacco Company, undertook as head of the Reynolds family and guardian of Smith, to bring about a family settlement, avoid unseemly litigation, and save the family's good name from being hauled through the courts.

Libby Holman's father was a lawyer. Repeated conferences between the immediate members of all the families concerned, together with their counsel, resulted in an agreement to a family settlement. It provided that the Cannon child should receive from the estate $1,500,000 and that Libby Holman and her child should receive a like amount; and that the balance, amounting to more than $25,000,000, should be placed in a trust fund to be known as the "Zachary Smith Reynolds Foundation," the income therefrom to be forever used for educational, charitable, and eleemosynary purposes in North Carolina. It was agreed that a tax of $2,000,000 should be paid to the State of North Carolina.

Because the rights of infants were involved, the agreement was submitted to the court for its approval, and authority was asked to work out the details under the court's future direction. But here an outsider entered and threw a bomb that wrecked the entire plan and opened the floodgates of litigation. It came about in this way. When Smith and his first wife separated, Joe Cannon, her father, petitioned the court to make his wife the guardian for their granddaughter's estate, and the Cabarrus Bank and Trust Company (of which he was then president) the co-guardian, for the sole purpose of keeping the accounts. Later he disposed of his interest in the Trust Company and became president of a competing bank. It was then that Charles Cannon, his estranged brother, acquired control of the Cabarrus Bank and Trust Company. After Smith's death, Charles Cannon and his bank, learning of the proposed family settlement, employed a staff of able lawyers and bitterly fought the court's approval of the family settlement and the proposed Zachary Smith Reynolds Foundation.

In court they argued that the Reno divorce was void; that the settlement on Smith's first wife and her child was improperly made and not binding even though approved by the court; hence the Cannon child was entitled to receive the entire estate and no family agreement could be made which deprived her of this fortune. A petition had been filed with the court setting out the terms of the *proposed* family settlement. The Cabarrus Bank and Trust Company opposed it, alleging that the Reno divorce was void; that Smith's effort to make a will in New York while under age was void; and that the original settlement giving the child $500,000 and her mother $500,000 for life, under all the circumstances, was void; and that therefore Anne Cannon Reynolds, 2nd, was entitled to all of the estate.

Judge Warlick held that the family settlement was proper and that the 25,000,000-dollar estate should form a foundation for the benefit of eleemosynary institutions in North Carolina; and, further, that Libby Holman and child should also receive $1,500,000. This family settlement had been agreed upon by all of the immediate members of the family, to wit, Libby Holman, W. N. Reynolds, Joe Cannon and his wife Annie L. Cannon, the three Reynolds children—brother and sisters of Smith Reynolds—and also by Libby Holman's father and counsel for her, the Reynolds family, and the Cannon family.

But here again the Cabarrus Bank and Trust Company took charge of the case and appealed it to the State Supreme Court. In its brief, the fact was restated that the Reno divorce was void; that the New York will was void, and that the Cabarrus Bank and Trust Company should be allowed to present the matter to the court that had made the original settlement and ask the court to vacate its order and give the entire estate to Anne Cannon Reynolds, 2nd. The court held that the proposed settlement could not be made as a family settlement or otherwise. One judge dissented, but the majority of the court held that a petition should be filed with the court in Forsyth County seeking to set aside the former settlement made before Smith's death, and observing, "The right of the minor to question the proceedings in Forsyth in the due and orderly manner prescribed by law is the point at issue, and that right has been improperly denied by the judgment rendered."

We then waited for the petition to be filed in Forsyth Court asking, as the court had instructed, that a motion be made to set aside the original order, but no such motion was ever made. Without consulting Joe Cannon, the grandfather of the infant, or Mrs. Annie L. Cannon, its co-guardian, who had the custody of the child, or Anne Cannon, the mother, or their attorneys, the Cabarrus Bank and Trust Company discourteously set about to make a settlement in the very teeth of the State Supreme Court's decision. It secured the co-operation of Polikoff and Graves, who were counsel for Libby Holman, by promising them 27½ per cent of the entire estate, when it well knew that under the decisions of the Supreme Court of the State and the Supreme Court of the United States, Anne Cannon Reynolds' divorce was not worth the paper it was written on. It proposed to give the Cannon baby 37½ per cent, and the Reynolds children 37½ per cent, but was told by the Reynolds heirs that they would accept it only upon condition that it was to be used for charitable and other causes as stipulated in the original proposal.

The Reynolds children, Richard J. Reynolds, Mary Reynolds Babcock, and Nancy Reynolds Bagley, adhered to their first agreement which was made with the parties in interest and submitted to the court for its approval, but which the Supreme Court declined to approve. As evidence of this they had already signed an agreement, and filed it with the court, which they have consistently lived up to and which reads as follows:

Winston-Salem, N. C. April 14, 1933.

Mr. W. N. Reynolds,
City.
Dear Uncle Will:

Having heretofore agreed between ourselves upon a common desire to establish, out of the trust funds created by the wills of our father and mother for the benefit of our brother, Smith Reynolds, to which we may now be entitled and of which we may hereafter obtain possession, a trust for charitable, benevolent and eleemosynary purposes in the State of North Carolina, we write to confirm that agreement.

It is our common intentions, as agreed between us, to create such a trust whenever our dominion over and title to such estates, in whole or in part, is conceded or judicially declared to be such as to legally enable and entitle us to do it.

Save for the purpose named, we do not expect to claim or receive any part of such estates, other than such sum as is necessary to reimburse us for expenses incurred.

The sole reason for our participation in the litigation now pending over this property, distasteful as it will doubtless be, is to do what we can to make effective this plan, thus honoring and perpetuating the memory of our brother, Smith.

We understand Mrs. Smith Reynolds and the mother and grandparents of Anne Cannon Reynolds, 2d, are in accord with this plan.

                    Affectionately,
                      Richard J. Reynolds
                      Mary Reynolds Babcock
                      Nancy Reynolds Bagley

The last paragraph of this letter tells the whole story: "We understand that Mrs. Smith Reynolds and the mother and grandparents of Anne Cannon Reynolds, 2d, are in accord with this plan."

The first that we knew of a flank movement was a petition filed in Forsyth not to set aside the original judgment as ordered by the Supreme Court but to divide the estate. We countered with an answer insisting that the Supreme Court's decree be carried out and that the lower court inquire into the original settlement.

In her answer filed in the case, Anne Cannon, speaking of her so-called divorce in Reno, said: "That soon after the first compromise settlement was approved by the Court Smith began to 'phone her at her father's home, where she and her child were living. Notwithstanding their separation she still loved him and hoped for a reconciliation. His attentions to her and the baby encouraged this hope. He invited her to come to the Reynolds family home, which she did, spending several days there. Soon thereafter, he seemed to change his attitude and began urging her to go to Reno and get a divorce. She told him she did not then want a divorce, but he insisted. Finally, he urged that she go with him to Reno, where, as he advised, she could get a divorce within six weeks and then return home. After much persuasion she finally consented, and he took her by plane to Reno. She was very nervous and sick after she reached Reno, and was physically unable to sign her name to the papers that the lawyer presented to her to sign. She continued sick, and was not at the trial, and the lawyer came to her room and asked her some questions, and then signed her name to the papers for her, ... She knew nothing of law, and followed and acted on Smith's advice. She had seen from the newspapers that one could go to Reno for six weeks and get a divorce and Smith told her that this was all that was necessary. She had no intention of giving up her home in Concord or of making her home in Nevada.

"That her sole and only purpose in going to Reno was to secure this divorce. She knew no one in Reno where she stayed at Riverside Hotel and Lazy Me Ranch, and she went to Reno intending to come back to her home and family in Concord as soon as the divorce was granted, and this she did.... That she did not know when she agreed to go with Smith to Reno to secure this divorce that he was engaged and intended to marry any other woman, and did not know that he was then under contract with Libby Holman to marry her as soon as this divorce could be secured, and did not learn until afterwards that the very day that the final decree in the divorce case was entered in Reno that he and Libby Holman secured a license to marry, and in a few days thereafter did marry."

Here was presented to the court a perfect case of a void judgment for divorce in Reno. The Supreme Court of the United States had expressly held such divorces void and the Supreme Court of North Carolina had also held that a divorce obtained in Reno under such circumstances was no divorce and that a second marriage was bigamous.

Anne Cannon further alleged that this petition, filed in Forsyth, had been filed at the instigation of the Cabarrus Bank and Trust Company, which had been appointed co-guardian solely to keep the accounts, and that its only interest in the proceedings was to get what money it could for itself and counsel. She called the court's attention to the fact that Charles Cannon, who was instigating this matter, did not speak to her father and cared nothing for her child. Upon this subject she told the court: "That it is a fact that the President of the Cabarrus Bank and Trust Company, who dominates and directs the action in this matter, and who became such officer after her father, J. F. Cannon, had it appointed co-guardian with the agreement above set forth, is C. A. Cannon, her Uncle; that he is not a part of the respondent's family circle, or interested in her family welfare. On the contrary, he lives immediately across the street from her parents' home where her child has lived since birth, and he has not been in the home for more than five years. That he and her father do not speak, and have not except on business for a number of years. That he has no family interest in her child...."

Here was positive, indisputable evidence that the Cabarrus Bank and Trust Company was an alien to the family and had no duty or authority except to file the motion to set aside the original decree. But the decision had already been agreed upon, and the court signed a long decree already prepared. We appealed the decision to the State Supreme Court, expecting of course that it would stand by its former decision that the interest of the child could not be bartered with, and that no family settlement could be made. But the Supreme Court abandoned its former decision and held that this family settlement was good even though the record showed that every member of the infant's family opposed it. By this stupid decision of the court, $25,000,000 was subverted from a charitable trust for the benefit of the people of North Carolina.

The Reynolds children have kept faith, and Wake Forest College is now beneficiary of that portion of the estate received by them. What a pity that the court would not allow the $25,000,000 to be set up as a foundation which the families had agreed upon rather than permit the juggling with the law under the guise of a family settlement and the diverting of the estate over the protest of the Anne Cannon family, the only real party in interest. Mr. and Mrs. Joe Cannon personally came into court, backed by an affidavit of Mr. W. N. Reynolds, and asked the court to allow my firm 5 per cent of the recovery as a fee (amounting to $500,000). But nothing could add integrity or dignity to the sorry affair.

The estate, at the death of Smith Reynolds, inventoried about $32,000,000. The state, it was agreed, should receive $2,000,000 in taxes, and under the first proposed settlement, agreed to by all of the families, this would have left $25,000,000 for the eleemosynary institutions of the state.

From the record no one can determine just how this miscarriage of justice was accomplished. The Cabarrus Bank and Trust Company certainly could lay no claim to being a part of the family, and the court's approval of its failure to file a motion to set aside the original decree and of its proceeding *vi et armis* to divide the estate under the guise of a family settlement when the family was not consulted, raises the query: "Is justice a farce?"

To get the Cabarrus Bank and Trust Company out of the case after settlement by the courts, we paid the bank over $100,000.

27

The Lassiter Case and Others

WHEN a counsel is given all the material facts and has opportunity to study the law applicable to a case, he should be reasonably certain of winning it before instituting suit. But the situation is reversed when he is employed to defend an action already started. Then it is "catch as catch can" to save his client from harm if possible.

I was cast into such a situation and put on the spot when Robert Lassiter, accompanied by a battery of lawyers from eastern Carolina, appeared in our office for help in what at first seemed a desperate and hopeless case against him. A suit had been brought in the Federal Court at Greensboro by a trust company, trustee, seeking to foreclose a deed of trust to satisfy an indebtedness of about $800,000 due by the Southern Aggregates Company, a corporation principally owned by Lassiter. The corporation had no money and little credit, and Lassiter was bankrupt. A court order had already been issued notifying Lassiter to appear and show cause why the property should not be sold to satisfy a just debt.

We began fighting for delay by first securing an order from Judge Hayes extending the time to answer this notice, so as to afford us time to learn the facts and prepare Lassister's defense, if he had any. We next secured from the court permission to have our auditors examine the records and correspondence of the corporation, which for that purpose were impounded with the clerk of the court.

The unfolding facts were not only surprising but amazing. Lassiter controlled the Southern Aggregates Company, which owned and operated the best rock quarries in North and South Carolina, and furnished crushed stone for highway construction and railroad ballast. Under the strain and stress of it all, Lassister not only lost a fortune, but his good health also.

During the days of his prosperity Lassister had given employment to and promoted two Ragland brothers and had put them in charge of the Southern Aggregates Company, making one of them president and the other general manager. This company had borrowed $800,000 from New York banks, secured by the deed of trust in question. In the general financial debacle of the early 1930's, the New York bankers grew panicky and offered to sell these notes at a great discount. The Raglands, sensing the ultimate come-back of the corporation, conceived the idea of buying the notes for their own personal benefit. To cover up the transaction, they had an uncle in Alabama purchase and take title from the bank in his name for them, without disclosing the deal to Lassiter and without making any effort to have the corporation buy the $800,000 indebtedness for $150,000, which the banks were offering to take.

When these facts were presented to the court, a receiver was appointed for the property. From time to time the Raglands offered to buy Lassiter out. They first offered him $150,000—then increased the amount to $300,000, but we declined the offers. After months of litigation, the judge ordered the corporation returned to Lassiter and the mortgage canceled, upon his reimbursing the Raglands the money actually invested in the purchase of the indebtedness, which he promptly borrowed and paid. By the end of the litigation the corporation was making big money and its holdings were worth $2,000,000. By winning this suit, Lassiter was lifted from work and placed in a position of financial affluence. I prepared the final draft of the brief—which so pleased Lassiter that he had several hundred copies printed for distribution.

A man who has been actively engaged in the general practice of the law for fifty years encounters all the problems that a varied clientele has to contend with. Many involve life and death, some the intimate affairs of the family; and others have to do with the numerous financial dealings between citizens and corporations.

Ocasionally a case arises that is out of the ordinary and requires the service of a detective. It was such a case that I was called upon to defend in 1911. The Security, Life and Annuity Company at Greensboro had written a double indemnity policy for $10,000 on the life of a man living in Cordele, Georgia. He was reported dead by accidental drowning in Lake Okeechobee, Florida.

Upon investigation the insurance company became suspicious as to his death and declined payment. In due course, suit was brought on the policy and I as general counsel for the company went to Cordele to defend the action. There I was met with indignation that payment had been refused on the policy. The widow with her weeds and children, and the best trial lawyer in town, were assembled for the trial. The atmosphere of the court was one of resentment that a foreign insurance company should have the audacity to contend that the poor widow and children were not entitled to the face value of the policy.

For three long days we struggled, trying to impeach the testimony of witnesses brought from Florida, who swore that they were on the lake in another boat and saw the deceased as he fell from his boat and was drowned. They had his hat and coat with them as silent testimony of his disappearance. There were even innuendos throughout the trial that the company should not contest a plain case like this when it had no supporting testimony.

The jury promptly decided for the widow, and judgment was signed for double the amount of the policy as the death was accidental, according to the testimony. We gave notice of an appeal to the Supreme Court and took leave of Cordele, where our presence was unwanted.

But this did not end the case. Our detectives were vigilant and before the case reached the Supreme Court for review, the deceased was located in New Orleans, where he was in hiding under an assumed name. We took pains to see that he was escorted to Cordele, Georgia, where the public might cast their visual organs upon the living impostor and the insurance company would be justified in its defense.

We have since wondered what became of the crepe worn by the widow during the trial.

In 1922 I was engaged for the defense of an unusual case. Jess Armfield, whose family were bankers and men of prominence in the industrial world, was operating a bank in Thomasville, North Carolina. During a depression which was then on, his bank closed. Soon it was rumored that Armfield, the president of the bank, had been lending its money, in violation of the banking laws of the state, to promote sawmills and other enterprises which he controlled. Indignation ran high among the depositors, and in the midst of it Armfield disappeared. The papers carried stories of the bank's failure and its president's disappearance.

The court appointed ex-Sheriff Finch receiver of the bank, and he began the liquidation. Several months passed and there was no word from Jess Armfield. Finally the report came that a man visiting in Mexico City had seen Armfield there. A furore arose to bring him back for trial. He was soon brought back and taken before Judge B. F. Long, who, to everyone's surprise, fixed his appearance bond at $90,000, an unprecedented amount. Upon Armfield's failure to make the bond, he was committed to jail in Lexington.

Jess Armfield's home was in Greensboro, and he had commuted back and forth between Greensboro and Thomasville, thirty miles away. His wife, Dion Armfield, employed me to defend him after he was placed in jail. I was never able to get much help from him for his defense, for he seemed confused and completely humiliated over having been brought back from Mexico and placed in jail to await trial. He presented a sad spectacle and apparently had few friends. His case seemed hopeless, except for such mitigating circumstances as might be developed in an effort to reduce his contemplated sentence.

I was urged to apply to the judge to reduce his bond so that he might be free to give aid to his counsel in preparing his defense. But here a question of strategy arose. Judge Long, who had fixed his bond at $90,000, was, I knew, a friend of the family, a learned judge, and an experienced lawyer. It was manifest that the Judge, in making Armfield's bond so unusually high thought it best for the defendant to be held in jail rather than to be let out on a smaller bond. The real question was if he wouldn't be better off at the trial, if he were brought into court from the jail, for this would attract public sympathy for him. I decided to let him stay in jail and before the trial ended it proved to be a wise move.

A special term of court was called for his trial and Judge B. F. Long was named presiding judge. The case lasted for a week, and during the first few days the State introduced the statute law forbidding officers of the bank to lend its money to themselves, and showed that the several corporations to which Armfield had loaned money were controlled by him at the time. The State then introduced the receiver of the bank, ex-Sheriff Finch, to show the insolvency of the concerns to which Armfield had made loans. The receiver was an able man and good trader. It developed that he had indirectly purchased assets of the bank and, the financial depression having eased, he would liquidate the bank and pay off its creditors. This opened a vista of light, and from then on I tried Finch for his double dealings with the assets of the bank and undertook to show that Armfield was a victim of a temporary depression. There was no charge of moral turpitude involved, but a breach of the banking laws of the state.

There was much wrangling among lawyers, and finally Emery Raper, leading counsel for the prosecution, jumped to his feet and with uplifted arms exclaimed to the judge that Mr. Brooks had already made thirty speeches to the jury. When offering and objecting to testimony I would argue the objections to the judge and he never stopped me, but consistently ruled against me. I noted an exception in the record of each of such rulings. By this time Armfield's continued journeys back and forth from jail got on the nerves of the crowded courthouse, and even the High Sheriff asked me if something couldn't be done to let him out of jail. The case was finally given to the jury and they promptly brought in a verdict of "Not Guilty."

I shall never forget the scene in the courtroom when the jury announced its verdict. The crowd cheered and Armfield's sister, who had sat in the bar of the court, jumped up and screamed, "Thank God the Armfield name has been cleared." There were many tears shed.

Although I was paid a satisfactory fee for defending the case, a very generous and unexpected contribution came weeks later from the family. One day, Bill Armfield a banker in Asheboro, came to my office and said that he and his father had not attended the trial because they thought it best to remain absent, but they had kept up with it and they deeply appreciated my services. He added that he and his father wished to show their appreciation, and he handed me a cheque for $1,500.

28

Lawyer Becomes Litigant

ALTHOUGH I have practiced law for fifty-seven years, I have never been a party to a lawsuit except once, and that was in an official capacity as one of three trustees. But since it resulted in the recovery of a million dollars after years of bitter litigation, it forms a part of my fifty years at the bar.

The case was a striking one, not only on account of the money at stake but because of the prominence of the parties involved. The suit was against H. Smith Richardson and Lunsford Richardson, Jr., as executors of the will of their father, Lunsford Richardson, Sr., and the Vick Chemical Company, a nationally known drug company.

In 1917 Lunsford Richardson, Sr., for whom I did no other law business before, and did none afterward, called on me to write his will. He was founder and sole owner of the Vick Chemical Company, had other large property interests in Greensboro, and was a ruling elder in the First Presbyterian Church of Greensboro, of which I was also a member. The practice of law presents a paradox in that people rarely select their counsel on account of a personal friendship but rather because of their confidence in a particular lawyer to best serve their purpose. Another characteristic of clients is that when a man comes to make his last will and testament he frequently turns aside from his regular attorney and selects another who knows nothing of his business and family affairs and confides to him how he wishes his earthly possessions disposed of at his death.

Mr. Richardson and I went over, item by item, the provisions which he wished incoporated in his will. As his fortune was principally in the Vick Chemical Company, which was then unincorporated, we adopted the method of treating it as one hundred units so as to facilitate its distribution among the beneficiaries by the use of percentages of the whole. To his two sons, Smith and Lunsford, Jr., he gave by the will and by previous gifts 62 per cent in order to assure their control of the business. To each of his daughters, Mrs. C. I. Carlson, Mrs. W. Y. Preyer, and Mrs. Chester Chapin, he gave in trust 10 per cent for life with remainder over to their respective children. The balance he gave to his wife, Mary Lynn Richardson, for life, under Item Fifth of the will, which reads as follows:

> I give and bequeath to my beloved wife, Mary Lynn Richardson, eight one-hundredths interest in the Vick Chemical Company. At the death of my said wife it is my desire that of the said eight one-hundredths interest so devised to her, three one-hundredths thereof shall be and become absolutely the property of the Trustees of the First Presbyterian Church, and the profits or dividends arising therefrom shall be used by the said Trustees for the benefit of Home and Foreign Missions and the benevolent causes of the church, in such proportion as the Trustees deem best. The remaining five one-hundredths interest I desire to be distributed equally among my five children, herein named, each receiving one share thereof in fee simple.

Lunsford Richardson was naturally a spiritual man and his wife was equally religious. She was the daughter of Jacob Henry Smith, a famous Presbyterian divine; three of her brothers were noted Presbyterian ministers and two of them distinguished educators. In drafting Item Fifth of the will, Mr. Richardson impressed upon me his desire to set up a trust for Home and Foreign Missions and other Benevolent Causes of his denomination. He said that while 3 per cent of his business then seemed a small portion of his estate, the Vick Chemical Company was making much money, was just in its infancy, and had an unlimited future; that this fund would in time, he felt sure, be very large and he wished it so arranged that through all the years to come these Causes in which he was so deeply interested would enjoy its benefits. He expressed the wish that the trustees of the First Presbyterian Church of Greensboro be named as his trustees to administer this trust for the benefit of these Causes and that it be distributed by them among the Benevolent Causes in their discretion. His designation of the trustees of the First Presbyterian Church of Greensboro was for the purpose of insuring a perpetuating body which would last through all time.

I notified Mr. Richardson after a rough draft of the will was made, and he asked if it would be agreeable to bring with him to go over the will his son, H. Smith Richardson. Accordingly, they came and the will was read in the presence of both of them, item by item, and Smith Richardson offered several suggestions, which were incorporated into the will.

Mr. Richardson died in August, 1919. The will was admitted to probate and a copy spread upon the minutes of the Vick Chemical Company. The two sons, Smith and Lunsford, Jr., and their mother, qualified as executors under the will. The Company, which had been incorporated in the meantime, had become extremely prosperous, and for the fiscal year ending June 30, 1923, its net earnings amounted to $2,194,282.35. In 1922, Smith Richardson, who had succeeded his father as president of the Company, and the other members of the family decided to buy the shares representing the three one-hundredths interest in which the widow, then living, had a life estate. The family agreed that the offer to buy should be made in writing by the widow, in her name, and that the other members of the family would furnish the money and that after she had acquired the Church's interest they would take over the stock from her and divide it among themselves, including also their mother's life interest in it. Accordingly, on November 10, 1922, Mrs. Mary Lynn Richardson addressed to the Clerk of Session, First Presbyterian Church, Greensboro, North Carolina, the following letter:

You will recall that Mr. Richardson, in his will, left to the 1st Pres. Church at my death, three one-hundredths of the stock of the Vick Chem. Co.—that is, 225 shares—"to become absolutely the property of the 1st Pres. Church, and the profits, or dividends arising therefrom, shall be used by the said Trustees for the benefit of Home and Foreign Missions and the benevolent causes of the church, in such proportion as the Trustees deem best."

I have been thinking a great deal lately, of this bequest, and wish to present to the Session my ideas thereon.

This stock will not come into the possession of the church until my death, but it seems to me that the church needs money now, more than it will later. In addition, I am very much interested in seeing that some part of the church which Mr. Richardson loved so well, be identified with his name and that this be done now, before those who knew, and loved, him have passed away.

In talking this over with my son, H. S. Richardson, he said it could be done, by the Vick Chem. Co. buying the rights to these 225 shares, if a price, mutually agreeable, could be arrived at.

I am also very much interested in Davidson College, and the family is now making gifts to the College, which will also become a memorial to Mr. R. Therefore, if this plan is carried out, I would wish: 1st. That at least $5000.00 of whatever price is agreed upon be given by the 1st Pres. Church to Davidson College, to be added to the L. Richardson Memorial Fund there.

2nd. That some part of the new church, into which I suppose this money will go, will bear Mr. R's name and be a permanent memorial to him.

3rd. Mr. Richardson's wishes were, that the income or profits from this stock go for the *benefit of Home and Foreign Missions and the Benevolent Causes of the Church. I feel, however, that he would thoroughly approve of this transaction provided these three causes should not suffer.*

Can anything be worked out along this line?

The above is merely a suggestion which I am glad to submit for your consideration.

Very truly yours,
Mary Lynn Richardson

The price offered for the 225 shares, including Mrs. Richardson's life estate, was $45,000, of which $5,000 was to go to Davidson College and the remainder to the First Presbyterian Church of Greensboro to be used in the erection of a new church. The transaction was handled by a committee of the First Presbyterian Church and after the sale had been negotiated the trustees were asked to consummate it. The trustees at that time were R. R. King, Sr., R. G. Vaughn, and George A. Grimsley. The trustees carelessly signed the transfer without knowing what its provisions were or without reading the will. The Home and Foreign Missions and other Benevolent Causes of the church never knew anything of this purported sale until seventeen years later after Mrs. Richardson died.

Later, Mr. Grimsley removed from Greensboro and resigned as trustee of the church. In 1932 I was named trustee in his stead.

---

* Emphasis supplied.

Two months after Mrs. Richardson's death on July 16, 1940, Judge Willis M. Everett of Atlanta, Chairman of the executive committee of Home Missions of the Presbyterian Church in the United States wrote the trustees to know when the benefits from this trust left by Mr. Richardson would become available to the Home and Foreign Missions and the Benevolent Causes. Mr. King, who was chairman of the Board of Trustees, turned the letter over to counsel for the Richardson family, who replied on September 23, 1940, that the stock had long since been sold to the Vick Chemical Company and that therefore the church had no claim against the Richardson family. Not satisfied with this response, Judge Everett came to Greensboro for a conference with the trustees under the will. He later gave a deposition in which he testified:

Mr. Brooks offered to resign as Trustee if Mr. King and Mr. Vaughn thought best, and have the court appoint other Trustees; but Mr. King and Mr. Vaughn said that they felt it was their duty to carry out the Will and intent of Mr. Lunsford Richardson, and they wanted to do whatever was right in the matter.... I explained that, in my opinion, the Will gave no interest or control of this bequest to the First Presbyterian Church but that the Trustees of the First Presbyterian Church were Trustees for Home and Foreign Missions and the Benevolent Causes of the church, and that, in my opinion, it was clearly their duty to demand of the Executors the delivery of this 3/100ths interest in the Vick Chemical Company. ... I told them that in my opinion, the attempted purchase of this remainder interest by the life tenant and the Executors who were administering the Estate of Mr. Richardson was, as I understood it, forbidden by the law and constituted a fraudulent transfer which the court would not sanction.

Following the conferences between the trustees and counsel for the Richardsons, Mr. King, on March 12 and June 4, 1941, wrote the two executors, Smith and Lunsford Richardson and the Vick Chemical Company, demanding an accounting. They declined to acknowledge any liability for an accounting and failed to disclose the real purchasers of the stock. The trustees then, in conjunction with various executive agencies of the church at large, engaged as counsel R. R. King, Sr., and the firm of Brooks, McLendon & Holderness, for the trustees of the First Presbyterian Church of Greensboro and the Executive Committee of Christian Education and Ministerial Relief; Charles G. Rose, of Fayetteville, North Carolina, for the Executive Committee of Religious Education and Publication and the Executive Committee of the Board of Trustees of the General Assembly's Training School for Lay Workers, Inc.; and Judge Willis M. Everett, of Atlanta, Georgia, and Brooks, McLendon & Holderness, for the Executive Committee of Home Missions.

In preparing the bill in equity, counsel realized that Mrs. Mary Lynn Richardson was of advanced age at the time of the transaction complained of, was not experienced in business, and had in nowise profited by the stock deal. Hence, in Article 27 of the bill in equity there was incorporated the following clause:

That the plaintiffs are informed and believe and therefore allege, that during the time of all transactions herein complained of Mrs. Mary Lynn Richardson, the widow, was of advanced age and not experienced in business matters and that she relied implicity upon the suggestions and advice of her sons Smith Richardson and Lunsford Richardson, and that all of her dealings as one of the executors and trustees and stockholders of the Vick Chemical Company were directed and approved by the defendants Smith Richardson and Lunsford Richardson.

In neither the complaint nor in any of the other documents filed with the court was Mrs. Richardson ever charged with any wrongdoing.

A thorough study of the principles of law applicable to the facts then known to the trustees had convinced counsel for the plaintiffs that the defendants could be held liable for an accounting to the plaintiffs on the following grounds:

1. A trust had been created by the terms of the will in favor of the benevolent causes of the Church and the defendants had breached their trust by unlawfully diverting these shares of stock from the purposes of the trust without the knowledge and consent of the beneficiaries;
2. The Trustees of the First Presbyterian Church had no power or authority under the terms of the will to sell the 225 shares to any party;
3. The Richardsons were Executors and Trustees under the will of their father in 1922, and their attempt to purchase these shares of stock which belonged to a beneficiary of the trust was fraudulent;
4. There was actual fraud on the part of the Richardsons in their attempt to acquire these shares of stock in that they misrepresented the real purchaser of the stock, they paid an inadequate price for the stock, and the offer of purchase contained a vital misquotation of the terms of the will.

Consequently, the complaint which was drawn and filed in the United States District Court for the Middle District of North Carolina at Greensboro contained allegations to support a recovery on all or any one or more of the grounds as listed above, with appropriate prayers for an accounting and for such other relief as might be just and proper.

Counsel for the plaintiffs were relying heavily on the decision of the Supreme Court of the United States in the case of *Michaud et al* v. *Girod et al* (4 How. 503), and upon the well established rule of trust law so clearly stated and explained in *Bogert on Trusts and Trustees* (Vol. 3 Sec. 493), as follows:

> Experience has shown the courts also that, in a large percentage of the cases where trustee and beneficiary have direct business dealings, the trustee gets an unfair advantage and uses his knowledge and influence for his private benefit.
> For these reasons, and because equity is anxious to protect and

foster fiduciary relations, chancery has built up a set of doctrines which restrict and guard business intercourse between the fiduciary and his principal. This control is not so severe as in the case of acts by a fiduciary which are to his private advantage and are done during the administration of the trust without direct dealing with the cestui. Those last named acts are always breaches of the fiduciary's duty of loyalty to the principal, and any advantages gained by the fiduciary thereby may always be taken from him, by way of constructure trust or otherwise. Fullness of disclosure, honesty of intentions, the payment of an adequate price, lack of damage to the cestui, are in no case excuses. The cestui may attack the transaction which was a breach of the duty of loyalty. Putting it in another way, the presumption of its fraudulent character is irrebuttable.

The *Michaud* v. *Girod* case was substantially analogous to the Richardson case for in that case two brothers who were executors under their father's will, and who wished to acquire for themselves a certain part of their father's estate, advertised the property for sale and had it bought in at the sale by a third party, who immediately transferred it back to them as individuals. In the *Michaud* v. *Girod* case the Supreme Court of the United States, in a very elaborate and unanimous opinion had held:

The conclusions to which we have come in this cause do not require from us any comment upon its facts.... But the morality and policy of the law, as it is administered in courts of equity, induce us to add, that those purchases were fraudulent and void, and may be declared to be so, without any further inquiry, upon the ground that they were made by the intervention of persons who were nominal buyers of the property for the purpose of conveying it to the executors. Such a transaction carries fraud upon the face of it. It matters not in such a case, whether the sales are made with or without the sanction of judicial authority or with ministerial exactness. The rule of equity is, in every code of jurisprudence with which we are acquainted, that a purchase by a trustee or agent of the particular property of which he has the sale, or in which he represents another, whether he has an interest in it or not—per interpositam personam—carries fraud on the face of it.

The defendants, through their counsel, Frazier & Frazier, R. M. Robinson, H. S. King, R. R. King, Jr., and C. R. Wharton, all of Greensboro, representing Smith Richardson and Lunsford Richardson as executors of their father's will, and Manly, Hendren & Womble, of Winston-Salem, Marion W. Smith, Richard K. Hines, and McCanless & Early, all of New York, representing the Vick Chemical Company, filed answers to the plaintiffs' complaint, in which they contended that the stock involved had been the absolute property of the First Presbyterian Church of Greensboro, unencumbered by any trust of any kind, and that the sale by the trustees had been an arms length transaction, made in good faith and for valuable consideration in accordance with the state and church laws applicable to the sale of church properties, and that, in any event, the plaintiffs' right to recover was barred by laches and by the statutes of limitation because the plaintiffs had waited too long after the alleged breach of trust and purchase occurred to make their claims and bring their suit.

After many pretrial maneuvers by both sides, including the taking of depositions and the filing and answering of interrogatories, and after a lengthy trial before Judge Johnson J. Hayes, District Judge, the District Court made its decision in favor of the plaintiffs, adopting the theory that the trustees had no power or authority under Mr. Richardson's will to sell the trust property, and that the purported sale, which was made without an order of court, was null and void.

The defendants had stated to the District Court during the arguments of counsel at the end of the trial that they were ready and willing to pay whatever amount, if any, they were legally responsible for, even though they would always feel that any judgment which might be rendered against them would be inequitable. Though basing his decision on a theory which did not require any finding of fraud, Judge Hayes in his Findings of Fact stated:

> ... The real purchaser, however, was H. S. Richardson (91 shares), Lunsford Richardson, Jr., (59 shares) and their three sisters (25 shares each). A plan had been formulated by these real purchasers by which they "had already agreed before the transaction was entered into to take over from the said Mary Lynn Richardson, either directly or through the Vick Chemical Company, the said stock interest that she was acquiring from the church or its trustees." In carrying out such plan, the real purchasers paid to Mrs. Richardson their pro rata part of $45,000, and she in turn paid such sum to the church.... Not until the true facts were established by the evidence in this trial was it known who the real purchasers of the remainder interest from the church or its trustees were.

And at the same time Judge Hayes held that "the charges of fraud against each and every defendant and Mrs. Mary Lynn Richardson are not sustained and are dismissed." It was apparent that Judge Hayes, who fully realized the importance of the case, not only to the parties themselves, but also to the First Presbyterian Church of Greensboro, hoped and expected that his decision in favor of the plaintiffs on a legalistic ground and his exoneration of the defendants from the charges of fraud would be acceptable to everyone and bring the case to an end. But not so.

The defendants gave notice of an appeal to the Circuit Court of Appeals in Richmond. The plaintiffs were only interested in recovering the stock and were content with the court's decree even though, whether right or wrong, the charges of fraud had been dismissed. The defendants, however, were still contending that they were not required to turn over the stock which Mr. Richardson had left in trust to the Causes of the church and continued their efforts to avoid having to account for the stock. The appeal to the Circuit Court of Appeals naturally carried with it the Opinion and Findings of Fact of Judge Hayes. The plaintiffs had no way of knowing which one of the four grounds charged in the complaint would be accepted by the Court of Appeals as a basis for its judgment, and consequently, the plaintiffs presented their full case to that court.

The Circuit Court of Appeals observed: "that the defendants had no fraudulent intent and honestly believed that they were acting lawfully does not affect the matter." In an elaborate opinion, this court held that the plaintiffs were entitled to recover from the Richardsons and the Vick Chemical Company the trust fund sought. The court held that "the sale was made in breach of the trust." Further, the court, in its Opinion, said:

... as a result of the diversion of the trust fund nothing has been received by the charities for which the trust was established in the will of testator.... [Mrs. Richardson paid the Session] $45,000 in cash, which she had received from her children for that purpose. She then transferred to her children, in accordance with the prior arrangement, the entire interest in the shares including her life estate as well as the remainder interest purchased from the trustees; ... There can be no question but that the sale was made, in breach of the trust, to obtain funds for the new church building, that it was made pursuant to a prior arrangement that the proceeds from the sale should be used for that purpose, and Mrs. Richardson and her children to whom the stock was transferred were parties to the arrangement.... The fact that the person taking the conveyances from the trustees was one of the executors, that the other two received transfers of the stock from her and that all were parties to the plan by which the stock was being diverted from the purposes of the trust, means that the transfer amounted to nothing.

The court also held that:

> The payment to the trustees were not used for the purposes of the trust, but was diverted to other purposes, viz., the building of a new church and the payment of a subscription by the Richardson family to Davidson College; and, as heretofore stated, the persons making the payment knew at the time that it was to be thus diverted. The trust certainly cannot be charged with the payment made to the trustees under such circumstances....

The plaintiffs naturally thought that this sweeping decision would at last end the matter, but not so. The defendants, still seeking to avoid an accounting for the trust fund, applied to the Supreme Court of the United States for a writ of certiorari to review the judgment of the Court of Appeals, but this application was denied.

The Circuit Court of Appeals in its decision held that the exact amount of recovery could not be fixed at that time because there was not sufficient evidence before the court as to what the amount of recovery should be. When the case came back to the District Court for a further hearing the defendants continued to fight against a recovery of any amount whatsoever on technical grounds relating to the many organizations and reorganizations to which Vick Chemical Company had been subjected in the interim since Mr. Richardson's death, and offered as a witness Professor Austin Scott, of Harvard Law School, author of "Scott on Trusts," in an effort to explain why some of the stock dividends should be credited to the account of the life tenant, Mrs. Richardson, rather than to the remaindermen, the Causes of the church. When Professor Scott had concluded his testimony, counsel for the plaintiffs asked him if, in his monumental book on trusts, he had not stated the rule to be exactly the reverse from that which he was then testifying. He replied, "Yes," but said that he was mistaken in his book. He was asked if he had advised all the subscribers to his book of this mistake. He replied, "No," and was dismissed as a witness. The atmosphere in the court was becoming a little frigid toward the defendants and they began to offer to compromise. They first offered $350,000; then raised the ante to $500,000; then to $750,000, but none of these offers was accepted, and finally a decree was entered, from which no appeal was taken by either the plaintiffs or the defendants, under which the plaintiffs recovered just a little more than $1,000,000.

When the final order was entered in the United States District Court on November 17, 1944, requiring the defendants to restore to the trust approximately $1,000,000, representing the value as of the date of Mrs. Richardson's death of the securities which had been unlawfully diverted plus interest at the rate of 6 per cent per annum from the date of Mrs. Richardson's death, it was thought by all concerned that the final chapter of this litigation had been closed. Such was not to be the case, and unfortunately it was kept alive and tried in the ecclesiastical courts for five long years and finally closed in June, 1950, nine years to a month after the action was formally instituted. The civil suit was against Smith and Lunsford Richardson as executors of their father's will. No one else was involved.

In May, 1946, the matter was first brought before the General Assembly of the Presbyterian Church in the United States, the highest court of this church, representing in one body all of its churches. This effort on the part of the Richardson family sought a withdrawal by the church court of the charges made in the civil courts. In accordance with the procedure of the General Assembly, this request for action was referred to a standing committee, composed of ministers and laymen, including lawyers and judges, who studied the matter in detail and who then reported their recommendations for action to the

General Assembly. The unanimous action taken by the 1946 General Assembly of the church was to commend the agencies for their diligence in looking after the interests of the church and to register its satisfaction with the civil courts' exonerations.

This action taken by the 1946 General Assembly of the church apparently did not satisfy the Richardsons, for on May 8, 1947, they sent to each commissioner of the 1947 General Assembly the following documents: A two-page letter requesting the appointment of "a committee with such powers as you deem proper to consider two subjects relating to the litigation of the L. Richardson Trust Fund"; a twenty-nine-page printed statement entitled: "The Strange Record of a Gift"; and a ten-page printed supplement "Giving Additional Information Concerning the Litigation of the L. Richardson Trust Fund and the Possible Effects of this Litigation Upon the Future Effectiveness of the Work of Our Church." Once again, the 1947 General Assembly referred the matter to a standing committee for the purpose of fully considering the charges and complaints of the Richardson family, and the action of this General Assembly was similar to that taken by the 1946 General Assembly.

Still the Richardsons desired to keep the matter before the public and the members of the church. On November 28, 1947, they sent a letter and a copy of the twenty-nine-page printed statement entitled "The Strange Record of a Gift" and the "Supplement" to each minister and elder in the Southern Presbyterian Church. In these documents each Session was requested to file the documents with its permanent records and to have the individual members inform themselves of the charges and the answers of the judges.

Thereafter, various Presbyteries sent overtures to the 1948 General Assembly requesting that similar action be taken as had been requested of the 1946 and 1947 General Assemblies by the Richardsons. For the third time, the matter was referred to a standing committee, composed of eminent ministers and laymen, including judges and lawyers, and for the third time the 1948 General Assembly took substantially the same action as its predecessors did.

The next step to be taken by the Richardsons in the trial of this matter before the ecclesiastical court was the preparation and transmittal on March 8, 1949, of a printed letter by Mr. Smith Richardson and Dr. Henry Louis Smith to each minister of the Presbyterian Church in the United States enclosing a seven-page printed article by Walter Lingle entitled "As I See It." The letter concluded with the statement that "only action now by the General Assembly can fully clear the good name of our Church." Additionally, several Presbyteries, including that of Charleston, South Carolina, requested that apologies be made and regrets expressed because of the charges made in the civil courts. Probably in view of the fact that the matter had been brought before three previous General Assemblies and had been carefully studied and considered by those bodies and still no result had been reached which was satisfactory to the Richardson family, the 1949 General Assembly adopted a motion "that a Judicial Commission be appointed to deliberate upon and conclude the business of the overtures and other papers before the Assembly growing out of the L. Richardson suit."

Such a Judicial Commission, composed of twenty-seven ministers and laymen, including eminent lawyers, met in Memphis, Tennessee, on October 24-27, 1949. After considering the statements and documents presented by the Richardson family and by the Benevolent Agencies, and after hearing statements made by members of the Richardson family and others who desired to be heard, the Judicial Commission handed down a unanimous report in which the following appears:

The Commission holds that the courts' findings and decrees dismissed all character charges and all charges of intentional fraud against H. Smith Richardson and Lunsford Richardson, Jr., and the Vick Chemical Company, and against Mrs. Mary Lynn Richardson if any were made against her. Since the courts that tried the case were courts of final and competent jurisdiction, the Commission holds that the findings and decrees should be given full faith and credit by all parties concerned and by the church at large.... The representative of the Richardson family declared to the Commission: "We are not asking these agencies to apologize to the Richardson family. We are not here asking for that, and we are not going to ask for it."... The Commission believes that the allegations made by the church agencies and trustees in this suit were made and prosecuted in good faith, and it also believes that no apology from our agencies need be forthcoming unless the agencies in good conscience feel constrained to make one. The Commission holds that the previous actions of the General Assembly, together with the findings of this Commission, should satisfactorily clear up and close this matter both for the Richardson family and for the church.

But the Judicial Commission apparently underestimated the persistence of the Richardsons, for they later showed they did not consider that the action of the Judicial Commission did "satisfactorily clear up and close this matter both for the Richardson family and for the church." An attorney of Charleston, South Carolina, was employed by the Richardsons to study the case and request further action of the Benevolent Agencies. This attorney prepared a twenty-two-page document for submission to the Agencies. This document constitutes what churchmen call an *apologia pro vita sua*. The attorney states quite frankly that the finding of the Court of Appeals in this case was that there had been committed "fraud-in-law," but argues at length that "fraud-in-law implies no moral turpitude, no dishonesty, no intent to do wrong and is totally different from fraud-in-fact which is intentional wrongdoing as the word fraud is commonly understood among ordinary men." In effect, this attorney made the plea to the Benevolent Agencies that their counsel, who were also members of their Board, during the trial of the action, and their successor attorneys, were unable to understand the legal significance of the facts and the opinions of the courts that passed upon this litigation and that for this reason the Agencies should now agree with Mr. Richardson's counsel's interpretation and expressly repudiate the action taken by their own counsel before the Judicial Commission.

On March 31, 1950, the Messrs. Richardson wrote to each of the members of the Benevolent Agencies and stated bluntly that they "and members of the General Assembly have been misinformed as to the meaning of the Decrees of the Civil Courts," and that:

> The purpose of this letter is not to prolong a controversy but to express this belief: that in order to "satisfactorily clear up and close this matter," both for the Richardson family and for our Church, your Committee should issue an official statement:
> 1) withdrawing these charges in a straight-forward manner;
> 2) explaining why your Committee has remained silent all these years; and
> 3) stating that there exists no additional evidence in your possession which, if brought to light, would further blacken our good name.

Soon thereafter the Presbytery of Charleston, of which this attorney was an active member, sent an overture to the 1950 General Assembly, seeking still further action. This overture requested the General Assembly to instruct its boards to explain (1) why they "remained silent when the final decree of the Courts was handed down," and (2) "that the character the charges repeated to members of the Assembly did not represent 'additional evidence which if brought to light would further blacken the character of the Richardson brothers.'" The similarity in wording between the action requested in the Richardson brothers' letter of March 31 and that of the overture is quite striking. The 1950 General Assembly, for the fifth time and, it is considered by all concerned, the last time, referred the matter to a standing committee and upon its recommendations unanimously approved the report of the Judicial Commission, which had held that no apologies were required.

Records of the Board of Trustees of the Trust established by Mr. Richardson in his will, as filed with the court, show that there has been distributed to the Benevolent Causes of the church that were so dear to Mr. Richardson's heart, for the period from the conclusion of the litigation in early 1945 until June, 1950, a total of over two hundred thousand dollars. In the years to come there will continue to be distributed by the Board of Trustees large sums of money for the advancement of the Kingdom. Nine years to the month have been required to conclude the prosecution and defense of this matter in the civil courts and in the ecclesiastical courts. "Time is God's mighty right arm of recompense."

The final chapter in this case was written by Judge Hayes, who knew all the facts of the case and the struggle that the plaintiffs had been to in securing a judgment for something over a million dollars.

When counsel for the plaintiffs filed their petition with the court for an allowance of counsel fees, Judge Hayes said that the petitioners only asked for $100,000 in fees but that he would gladly have granted an application for $200,000 if the suit had involved ordinary individuals. During the course of this hearing Judge Hayes, who is also an eminent churchman, very aptly sized up the situation when he made the following pertinent statement:

The leaders of the Presbyterian Church of the South were confronted with a very serious problem of policy, too, that is whether it would be wiser to let the thing go and take chances on getting something more in the future in some other way, or whether it would be better to chase this thing out. I can see how matters of policy entered into it, but I have seen it from the standpoint of both plaintiff and defendants and I am firmly convinced today, as I have been ever since I made a study of the case, that the representatives of the Presbyterian Church of the South would have been derelict in their duty if they had not prosecuted this suit. There is not a shadow of doubt in my mind about the fact that the testator intended for this three one-hundredths interest to go to the beneficial causes of the Church, and certainly endeavored to fix it so that nothing could prevent that taking place.... It is unfortunate that this lengthy litigation had to be resorted to to carry out the intention of the testator....

In connection with that, the Executors contended that it was their desire to carry out the will and intention of the testator. They should not have any grievance. They found out what the Court of final jurisdiction has said, and they should welcome the opportunity of carrying out the desire of the testator. If the man who creates it shall not have some movement over the channels through which it should go, it is a poor incentive for a man to make money, and they should approve.

... recovery by the plaintiffs would have been impossible but for the manner in which the case was *studied, prepared* and *presented* * in Court by the petitioners.

I stated to the court that I would not accept any portion of the fee allowed my firm but, instead, would donate the same to the Causes mentioned in Mr. Richardson's will, and this I did.

Throughout this long and disagreeable litigation our sole purpose was to keep faith with Mr. Lunsford Richardson, Sr., and to see to it, as trustees under his will, that his trust would be faithfully and honestly carried out and that the Home and Foreign Missions and Benevolent Causes of the church should

---

* Emphasis supplied.

not be deprived of their just estate. We realized that it would be a long and unpleasant litigation but there was no choice. We felt that we owed a duty to the memory of Mr. Richardson and an obligation as trustees under his will, and were determined to keep faith with the Home and Foreign Missions and Benevolent Causes of the church.

29

The Romance of the Cigarette

NORTH CAROLINA was the first state in the Union to discover the process of curing leaf tobacco to produce a bright color. The discovery, which made possible a "bright tobacco" especially suited to the manufacture of cigarettes, has made tobacco a luxury throughout the civilized world. Through the development of the cigarette, millions of dollars have been made, and tobacco as an agricultural phenomenon challenges all comparison.

The discovery of how to produce bright tobacco and the evolution of the cigarette have occurred in my lifetime, and the romance of the cigarette has touched my life closely.

That section of the state which first produced the bright leaf, together with the adjacent counties in Virginia, is known as the Old Bright Tobacco Belt, and comprises two tiers of counties lying in the northern part of piedmont North Carolina: Surry, Stokes, Forsyth, Rockingham, Guilford, Caswell, Alamance, Orange, Person, Durham, Granville, and Vance. These counties produce a bright tobacco that is mild, with a sweet aroma, which has continued to serve as a basis for the manufacture of cigarettes.

Reared on a tobacco plantation in the Old Belt, I was personally familiar with the culture of tobacco from the plant bed of the seed through all the stages of cultivating, curing, and marketing. I can never forget the many trips I made hauling tobacco thirty miles through muddy roads, by wagon, to the Danville, Virginia, market, and there saw the Trust buy it at starvation prices. Danville, then and until 1919, was the greatest bright tobacco market in the industry. When I was sixteen years old, the Durham Bull Tobacco Company gave me an order to buy for them 100,000 pounds of leaf tobacco on the Roxboro market.

Later I was almost equally familiar with other phases of the tobacco industry. All of the nationally known figures of the American Tobacco Company and of the leading companies resulting from the dissolved trust—Liggett & Myers, American, Lorillard, and Reynolds—I knew personally. The Reynolds Tobacco Company, as already mentioned, offered in 1908 to make me its general counsel.

Politically, the American Tobacco Trust was an issue in every campaign in which I took an active part until its dissolution in 1911. Thirty years later, the American, Reynolds, Liggett & Myers, and Lorillard companies were indicted in Lexington, Kentucky, for violation of the Anti-Trust Act, and in a trial that lasted eight months my firm was counsel for the Reynolds Company. S. Clay Williams was chairman of the board of the Reynolds Company and had charge of its defense. Clay Williams, as he was known, went from my law firm in 1917 as assistant general counsel of this company. Through the years, on account of his great ability, he was promoted to its presidency and later was made chairman of its board.

To me, the story of tobacco in America is one of the most important and fascinating stories in our history. It is not generally known that the "bewitching vegetable" found by Columbus and by Sir Walter Raleigh's agents on Roanoke Island was a tobacco different from that introduced by Rolfe in 1612. The tobacco seed which he imported was a species known as the Aranoko, a "sweet tobacco." This sweet tobacco was destined to become known as the "golden weed," which goes into the manufacture of present-day cigarettes.

One of the most remarkable facts connected with the culture and curing of tobacco is that it took two hundred and fifty years for the tobacco planters to find out how to cure tobacco bright. It is an interesting story how the early planters in Virginia struggled to grow and cure a bright leaf by various processes such as hanging the plants in ricks to be cured by air, or, later, hanging the plants in barns and building log fires under them so that the heat and smoke would cure them. But still the leaf would be dark and bitter and would taste strongly of nicotine. This tobacco was suitable for chewing, and there was a growing demand for it in England, France, and Spain.

It was not until 1856 that the Slade brothers in Caswell County, North Carolina, successfully used charcoal to cure a large quantity of tobacco bright. There is a curious story connected with this discovery. A sleepy-headed Negro slave had been tending the tobacco barn on a rainy night and almost let the fire go out. The wood was wet, and so he hastily got some charcoal from a pit near by and renewed the fire with it. The sudden dry heat cured the tobacco to a bright yellow. This result created a sensation in that section of the state, and North Carolina has since placed a historical marker at the Slade home to commemorate it.

The phenomenon had been accomplished by the use of charcoal, but it was also discovered that the source of heat was not the entire answer, and that to produce bright tobacco, the plant should be grown on a light sandy soil underlaid with a yellow subsoil.

The Civil War, soon following this discovery, checked its general use, but after the war the bright tobacco culture expanded enormously. In 1871 (the year I was born) Major R. L. Ragland of Hyco, Virginia, only seven miles from my home in Person County, encouraged the use of flues in the curing of tobacco. The perfected flue, developed from an earlier invention which was never used to any extent, became the standard, and was substantially the same as that now employed throughout the country. The mechanism of the flue is so simple that it is amazing to realize that for two and a half centuries it baffled the ingenuity of man.

But now that the golden leaf could be cured, the entire story of tobacco changed, and its culture shifted from the Virginia lowlands to piedmont North Carolina and Virginia, a territory comprising an area one hundred miles wide and one hundred and fifty miles long, lying on either side of the dividing line between North Carolina and Virginia.

The coming of the bright leaf ushered in a trade in smoking tobacco and later in the cigarette. Durham, North Carolina, was to become the headquarters in this change, and a number of country boys moved in and took over. The first to establish a smoking tobacco factory in Durham was John Ruffin Green, about 1860. He and I were cousins, born in the same house in Person County, which my grandfather purchased from his father, Squire Green, when he removed his family to Durham. Green's middle name, Ruffin, was taken from the great Chief Justice Thomas Ruffin, who lived in an adjoining county. Green organized a small factory in Durham and adopted as his brand the name "Bull Durham," and had a picture of the bull painted on a sheet-iron slab.

One of the last events in the unhappy Civil War was enacted near Durham, and, by an interesting chain of circumstances, the surrender of General Joseph E. Johnston to Sherman resulted in making Durham—a little village—into a renowned city, and the "Bull Durham" into a world-wide product. While negotiations for surrender were in progress, Union soldiers descended upon Green's warehouse, in which he had stored quantities of granulated Bull Durham smoking tobacco, and stripped it. Green naturally felt that he had been ruined, but here again the fates came to his rescue. The Union soldiers, with their haversacks packed with tobacco, returned to their homes, and soon began writing him for more tobacco! His customers increased so rapidly that he needed more capital to meet the demands. He chose as his partner W. T. Blackwell, who turned out to be a genius in the tobacco business.

Blackwell also came from Person County about five miles from my home. Later Green died, and Blackwell purchased from his estate his interest in the business for $2,000 and took as a partner Julian S. Carr, who became a master salesman. Under the firm name of W. T. Blackwell & Company the business prospered to an unbelievable degree. The firm adopted the likeness of a more virile bull, designed by Reuben Rink (pseudonym of J. G. Koerner, of Kernersville), and sign painters carried it to every state in the Union and to a number of foreign countries. It was even said that the picture of this bull was painted on the pyramids of Egypt.

The success of W. T. Blackwell & Company was phenomenal, and riches poured in. The virility of the new bull was aptly illustrated in their trademark, with all of the bull's credentials in view and with the Liberty Bell, tied on with an American flag, hanging as a pendant from his neck. A humorist of the time said that you could tell the dividing line between the east and the west by the position of the bull—painted on the farther side of the fence, in the east, and on the nearer side, in the west. The Blackwell interests had litigation lasting fifteen years, in the state and Federal courts, over the "Bull Durham" trademark, in which it is said they spent $100,000 in lawyers' fees.

Blackwell realized that with Bull Durham's success, it was necessary to have a leaf tobacco market in Durham so that farmers could have a ready market. He therefore built the first two warehouses that were erected in North Carolina. To operate the first (built in 1871) he selected Henry A. Reams, and for the second Alexander Walker, both from Person County and our neighbors.

In 1874 the Dukes moved into Durham from their little farm in Orange County, about forty miles from my home, and engaged at first in a small way in manufacturing tobacco. The firm became known as W. Duke Sons & Company, comprised of the father, Washington Duke, and his sons, known as Buck, Ben, and Brodie. The "& Company" was George W. Watts, who acted as treasurer. This company succeeded from the start and engaged in the manufacture of plug, smoking tobacco, and snuff.

In 1881 J. B. Duke, who had become the driving force in the firm, engaged in the manufacture of cigarettes in a small way. There is an interesting story of how he acquired, on a reduced royalty basis, the Bonsack machine for making cigarettes and greatly improved it. James A. Bonsack of Virginia had developed a machine, and, although crude, it turned out to be a great labor saver and made of the Dukes real competitors in the business. Cigarettes were not new to the trade; they had been manufactured for years under various brands by manufacturers such as Allen & Ginter of Richmond, Virginia, and others. But up till then cigarettes had been made by hand—an expensive and slow process. The manufacturers used largely tobacco imported from Turkey, which gave the cigarettes a pleasant aroma. Duke's Bonsack machine, with added improvements, made cigarettes cheaper, but the same required content of foreign leaf continued.

In the 1880's a trade war was engaged in between the leading cigarette manufacturers, and, as was the custom of the times, no holds were barred. In this war the Dukes sought in every way to put the Bull Durham Company out of business, but at this time it was too well entrenched to be dislodged.

In 1890 the Dukes formed the American Tobacco Company and absorbed the remaining big companies which had survived the trade war, including the Bull Durham plant, which was purchased in 1899. Powerful and ruthless as was this octopus, its chief business was still in plug tobacco, snuff, and smoking tobacco. Up to the time of the dissolution of the monopoly in 1911, the value of cigarettes manufactured was relatively small.

It was not until 1913 that W. N. Reynolds of the Reynolds Tobacco Company discovered that the burley tobacco of Kentucky and Tennessee could be treated and used instead of Turkish tobacco as a basis for cigarettes. The announcement of this discovery created consternation in the tobacco business, but all manufacturers soon made use of it. At the time of this change, the records show that the total sale of cigarettes in this country amounted to only fifteen billion cigarettes a year.

A very small percentage of Turkish tobacco is still used by some of the manufacturers of cigarettes. Turkish tobacco is also being grown in North Carolina, and this is increasingly being used in place of tobacco imported from Turkey.

The name "Camel" was adopted by the Reynolds Company as a name for their cigarettes, and here we have another interesting story. When deciding upon a name, R. J. Reynolds, the founder of the Reynolds Tobacco Company, noted that the Turkish tobacco had to be brought on camels across the country to a seaport, and remarked that this was a short name and an appropriate one, and thus came the trade name "Camels."

With the discovery that burley could be used instead of Turkish tobacco, and with the introduction of new and improved mechanisms, the manufacture and sale of cigarettes began to increase at an incredible speed. Women began to smoke them, and it became fashionable to carry them in one's pocket or handbag. The cigarette made its way into the mansion and the log cabin and was eagerly sought after by soldiers, sailors, and generals alike. They were bootlegged in Germany during the Second World War at one dollar a pack, or more, and were exchanged for the favor of the women. Around the world cigarettes are now firmly entrenched in most households and in the pockets of every smoker able to have them.

The volume of cigarettes sold by American companies staggers the imagination. According to government reports for the year 1948 the number sold was 387 billion, and the tax paid was $1,000,208,000.

30

Looking Backward

MY ancestral tree was rooted in Massachusetts, whence my forebears early trekked down to Virginia, and about 1790 moved over to North Carolina. They were a sturdy lot, who wholeheartedly followed Washington. To such, Jefferson's teachings naturally appealed, and from then on they were ardent Democrats. It is often said, with much truth, that we usually embrace the political faith of our fathers. In my case, born in the wake of the Civil War and Reconstruction, it was inevitable that I should be a Democrat, imbued with the hatred of the Republican party and vehement dislike of Lincoln, whom the South then regarded as the author and finisher of its misfortunes. The term "dam yankee" was pronounced as one word and employed as an expression of contempt, especially by those who lived in the trail of Sherman's ruthless army.

It is intriguing and astonishing to recall how many things one learns and unlearns in a long lifetime. The education of Aubrey Brooks about the *causa causans* and personalities of the War Between the States began when I read the papers and letters of President Lincoln contained in a government publication sent me by my friend Congressman Kitchin. This stimulated my search for the naked truth about the Great Conflict and the leading actors on both sides. As a result I first learned that the great masses of the people, both North and South, did not want war, and that it was incited by a few Northern fanatics and brought to an issue of arms by a limited number of hot-headed southerners in South Carolina, the Mississippi Delta, and Alabama.

The next and most astonishing thing I learned was that Lincoln was not an enemy of the South, did not at first want to abolish slavery and destroy the property value in them, but advocated Congress's passing a bill paying $400 per person to the slave owners. I also learned that historians agreed that Lincoln's assassination took away the South's best friend in the Federal Government, and that he was bitterly opposed to any policy of reconstruction in the South.

But my greatest amazement came when I learned that he was at heart a Jeffersonian democrat, and had so stated in a letter in 1859 addressed to a committee in Boston celebrating the birthday of Jefferson, to which he had been invited to speak. He wrote:

To H. L. Pierce and Others.

Springfield, Ill., April 6, 1859.

Gentlemen:—Your kind note inviting me to attend a festival in Boston, on the 28th instant, in honor of the birthday of Thomas Jefferson, was duly received. My engagements are such that I cannot come.

Bearing in mind that about seventy years ago two great political parties were first formed in this country, that Thomas Jefferson was the head of one of them and Boston the headquarters of the other, it is both curious and interesting that those supposed to descend politically from the party opposed to Jefferson should now be celebrating his birthday in their own original seat of empire, while those claiming political descent from him have nearly ceased to breathe his name everywhere.

Remembering, too, that the Jefferson party formed upon the supposed superior devotion to the personal rights of men, holding the rights of property to be secondary only, and greatly inferior, and assuming that the so-called Democracy of to-day are the Jefferson, and their opponents the anti-Jefferson party, it will be equally interesting to note how completely the two have changed hands as to the principle upon which they were originally supposed to be divided. The Democracy of to-day hold the liberty of one man to be absolutely nothing, when in conflict with another man's right of property; Republicans, on the contrary, are for both the man and the dollar, but in case of conflict the man before the dollar.

I remember being once much amused at seeing two partially intoxicated men engaged in a fight with their great-coats on, which fight, after a long and rather harmless contest, ended in each having fought himself out of his own coat and into that of the other. If the two leading parties of this day are really identical with the two in the days of Jefferson and Adams, they have performed the same feat as the two drunken men.

But, soberly, it is now no child's play to save the principles of Jefferson from total overthrow in this nation. One would state with great confidence that he could convince any sane child that the simpler propositions of Euclid are true; but nevertheless he would fail, utterly, with one who should deny the definitions and axioms.

The principles of Jefferson are the definitions and axioms of free society. And yet they are denied and evaded, with no small show of success. One dashingly calls them "glittering generalities." Another bluntly calls them "self-evident lies" and others insidiously argue that they apply to "superior races." These expressions, differing in form, are identical in object and effect—the supplanting the principles of free government, and restoring those of classification, caste, and legitimacy. They would delight a convocation of crowned heads plotting against the people. They are the vanguard, the miners and sappers of returning despotism. We must repulse them, or they will subjugate us. This is a world of compensation; and he who would be no slave must consent to have no slave. Those who deny freedom to others deserve it not for themselves, and, under a just God, cannot long retain it. All honor to Jefferson—to the man, who, in the concrete pressure of a struggle for national independence by a single people, had the coolness, forecast, and capacity to introduce into a merely revolutionary document an abstract truth, applicable to all men and all times, and so embalm it there that to-day and in all coming days it shall be a rebuke and a stumbling-block to the very harbingers of reappearing tyranny and oppression.

Your obedient servant,

A. LINCOLN.

I was to learn that even General Sherman, who declared that "War is Hell," and proceeded to verify it in his march through Georgia to the sea, had some virtues to his credit. When General Johnston surrendered to him near Durham, he dictated such liberal terms of peace that the government in Washington, under the diabolical influence of the sadist—Thad Stevens—repudiated it.

In youth my political views were inherited, and I consequently embraced blindly the teachings of the Monticello idol. Through the intervening years I have diligently studied the political philosophy of America's two supreme geniuses in statesmanship—Jefferson and Hamilton. The respective schools of thought established by them in the dawn of our Republic still teach the essential differences to be found in a democratic form of government, and every political party employs one or the other as the touchstone of its belief.

The heart of Jefferson's democratic creed, "Equal rights to all and special privileges to none," was epitomized and made immortal by Lincoln's declaration for "a government of the people, by the people, for the people." The observations and experiences of half a century have confirmed my belief that liberty, equality, and justice among men can be attained and preserved only in a government which rests upon the consent of the governed, freely expressed.

The concepts of a democratic state, as taught by Jefferson,

defended by Jackson, fought for by Lincoln, exemplified by Wilson's New Freedom, and extended by Roosevelt's New Deal, have, in my opinion, forever ended the Hamiltonian theory of overlordship in governments everywhere. World movements in the last decade have created an irresistible undertow by organized society for more democracy, not less. The issue is fast forming between socialized democracy as a minimum of government control and Russian communism as a maximum. The days of kings and despots are numbered.

I began with Bryan, supported Wilson, and stayed with Roosevelt. I was not deluded into thinking any one of them perfect, nor did I approve of all their ideas. Bryan had the biggest heart, Wilson the best brain, and Roosevelt the greatest capacity for leadership. But whatever their differences and defects, and notwithstanding the shifting issues from time to time, they each were followers of Jefferson, and fought in their own ways to make this nation a true democracy, freed from capital cannibalism, and open to the common man to enjoy life, liberty, and the pursuit of happiness.

In the state I aligned myself with Will and Claude Kitchin, Walter Clark, and Josephus Daniels, the four ablest and most consistent advocates of liberal democracy. Walter Clark led all the statesmen of the South in his advocacy of legislation and judicial and social reforms, while Claude Kitchin, as chairman of the Ways and Means Committee of Congress, made a national reputation as perhaps the greatest debater for democracy of his generation.

I vividly recall the experiences of my days at the University Law School under Dr. Manning and Chief Justice Shepherd. My law class graduated twenty-one. A number of these became eminent. Howard Foushee of Durham and Harry Whedbee of Greenville became superior court judges; E. Y. Webb of

Shelby was a long while a member of Congress and U. S. District Court Judge for Western North Carolina; Hallett Ward of Little Washington became a congressman; and H. H. Covington, the brightest man in the class and the wildest, soon quit the law and became a distinguished Episcopal minister. W. A. Devin of Oxford is now a justice of the Supreme Court of North Carolina. Larry Moore of New Bern and several others also distinguished themselves.

I still recall Judge Shepherd's admonition to the class when we graduated: "Young gentlemen," said he, "when you go to the bar it will seem a long and hard road to the top but you will be surprised in the course of ten years, if you keep your place in the struggle, how nearly you will become one of the leaders of the bar. Don't ever complain if you don't feel well, and never air your complaints for that will only distress your friends and please your enemies."

My retirement in 1908 from the political arena as an aspirant for office did not dampen my ardor for the success of democratic causes and candidates. In every campaign since then I have taken an active part in party politics. But my adherence to the practice of law, employment as counsel for corporations, and especially my activity in the organization and general counselship for life and fire insurance companies, caused some of my democratic friends to conclude that I had at last been taken over by "Big Business." The truth was that I felt I could best serve my state, as well as myself, by giving proper counsel to organized wealth in building up the state. To this end, I maintained an office for the general practice, and declined more than one offer to become a "kept" lawyer of any one corporation, regardless of the financial inducements. In 1914 I was made president of the newly established Greensboro Golf Club, and in 1916 I was elected chairman of the Greensboro Chamber of Commerce. In 1917 I was president of the North Carolina Bar Association.

In 1944 the University of North Carolina Press published my biography of Chief Justice Walter Clark. My admiration for his distinguished service in the administration of justice in North Carolina and for his contribution to the progressive thought of the South induced me to write it. Later two volumes of the papers of Walter Clark were collected, with the aid of Hugh Talmage Lefler of the University of North Carolina, and were published in 1948 and 1950. They were motivated by my conviction that Clark's services as jurist and statesman had been neglected and that time and events have proved the truth of his thinking.

Looking back over the years for half a century, I see them, for me personally, as years of great adventure, some success, and much happiness. To the people of my state the same years have witnessed transcendent accomplishment in welfare and wealth, progress and prosperity, that staggers the imagination. It has been a great joy to me to see North Carolina come out of the doldrums of poverty following the ravages of the Civil War and take its stand proudly among the great states of the nation. I am proud to have had a small part in its development and in making it a fit habitation for all of its citizens. I cannot quit the subject without recalling the remarks of an old friend of years ago, Colonel John R. Webster. He was recovering from a slight stroke when I met him one day on the street. I said to him, "Colonel, I am glad to see you out and looking so well." "Brother Brooks" (as he was wont to address me), he replied, "I know that my days are numbered. I am not afraid to die, but so many things are going on I hate to leave them all."

31

The Afternoon of Life

Our philosophy of life either consciously or unconsciously shapes our thinking and forms our attitude toward life, our fellows, and our future. Emerson's essay on "Contentment" increased his fame; Grayson's "Adventures in Contentment" brought pleasure to thousands. Many others have descanted upon the subject of contentment, but it still remains an iridescent vision and baffles a complete definition. Doubtless there is no such thing as perfect contentment in this mundane life; yet its approximation is one of the noblest aspirations of the soul. The ever-present question is: How can it be attained and preserved? The answer is intensely personal and depends upon the individual's reaction to the ultimate balancing of his ambitions, hopes, and successes with his failures and fears, coupled with his requited or unrequited love.

Fortunately, contentment is no problem for youth and of little concern to middle age. It begins to loom as we pass the meridian of life and assumes increasing proportions as time beckons us to lay down one by one the cares and responsibilities of an active and creative life. Artemus Ward said, "It is not so hard to take things as they come, but the hell of it is to turn them loose as they go." From observation and experience I am persuaded that one of the most difficult things in life is to withdraw gracefully and happily from active participation in the daily affairs which for so long have been one's life blood.

Volumes have been written about how to retire and be contented. There is no such thing. Retirement, the dream of every professional and business man, leaves a vacuum that must be filled. It presumes a competency to take care of the rainy days, but the spirit of man demands more than financial security. Unhappily this truth is usually learned too late after the "bitch goddess success" has lured the soul away from the paths of tranquility and contentment. The experience of mankind seems to teach that to enjoy a contented mind and continual feast one must begin early in life to accumulate those intangible assets which in advancing years constitute a bank account for spare time, such as love of reading, art, music, and travel, fondness for outdoor life, fishing, and hunting. In a way, I have tried to practice what I preach.

The location and construction of a forty-acre artificial lake is as interesting and as engaging as planning and building a home. To stock a lake properly with suitable fish of differing varieties that will thrive together requires a study of the different species of game fish suitable to an upland lake, their habits and food requirements. This piscatorial realm is a world of its own, and when we take into account the complex subject of fish tackle, rods, reels, lines, lures, and flies by the dozens, it becomes as engaging and involved as an important lawsuit—and as uncertain. Taking a bass or bream on a fly with a four-ounce rod is entertaining, and I have so spent many carefree happy hours on my lake. For beginners and for those who are too "busy" with things less important to cultivate the art of casting a fly or other lure, there is still open to them the simple process of a pole, line, cork, sinker, hook, and worm. This is what the elite fisherman calls, in the South, "nigger fishing." The story is told of an old Negro who, while sitting on the bank of a wooded stream fishing, hooked a big catfish and, with a swing of his long reed pole, took him over his head and into the bushes behind. The fish, thrown free of the hook, floundered in an effort to get back to the water. Whereupon, the old man put his foot on top of the fish and addressed him thus: "Mr. Catfish, don't be so excited and try to get away from me. All I'se going to do to you is to gut you."

The fishing habit is akin to other habits, and to the ambitious it may become an obsession like making money—the larger the return the better you like it. This leads us in business to play for bigger stakes and bigger fish. I never believed in doing things halfway; hence I have responded to the call to fish for landlocked salmon and togue in the Grand Lakes in Maine, for sailfish in the Gulf Stream off the Florida Keys, for tarpon at Boca Grande, and last but not least, for rainbow trout in Canada.

But since fishing is seasonal, largely limited to the springtime, one should look in his kit of outdoor pleasures for other hobbies on other leisure days, such as shooting quail and duck and fox hunting. I have purposely listed the sports which I know most about and which have given me the greatest pleasure and surcease from the cares of an active law practice, and still give more promise of pleasure and contentment for my remaining future. A very real but intangible asset is the thrilling experiences enjoyed along the way, carefully preserved in the storehouse of my memory—there to be taken out on the least excuse. Never can I forget the many seasons in years past that I spent shooting on Currituck Sound when at sunrise the flight of ducks and geese would cloud the sky and there was practically no bag limit.

Unfortunately, so-called civilization, with its airplanes, good roads, and the automobiles, has tended to urbanize life at the expense of the sportsman. But to those who enjoy the chase, a pack of good fox hounds on a clear crisp morning will lift you out of yourself, banish every care and fill your soul with music. For years, I have kept a pack of Walker fox hounds at my lake. For centuries, fox hunting has been a sport for both kings and peasants, rich and poor, high and low alike.

Lord Halifax once said he had rather be master of the hounds than Prime Minister of England. Wellington, on his campaign in Belgium against Napoleon, took his pack of hounds with him and it is recorded that shortly before the Battle of Waterloo his hounds chased a fox through the enemy's lines and he followed on horseback to the kill. When an attendant warned of the danger, Wellington replied, "Wherever my hounds lead, I follow." He was allowed to return to his army unharmed.

32

The Law's Final Decree

HOOKER wrote: "Of Law there can be no less acknowledged than that her seat is the bosom of God, her voice the harmony of the world. All things in heaven and earth do her homage,—the very least as feeling her care, and the greatest as not exempted from her power."

The final chapter in all litigation embraces the law's conclusions; even so does the law of life write its decree, as summing up the pros and cons of this earthly struggle. The doctrine of works plays a major role, but at last Providence writes the decree. The fates have been exceedingly kind and merciful to me, and this *au revoir* is intended to record my appreciation of their blessings which have been greater than my deserts.

I came into this world during reconstruction following the Civil War. I have witnessed the Spanish-American War and have lived through two world wars and am now in a world where warring humanity is again on the march. Notwithstanding, I am persuaded that the world today offers more hope for freedom and justice to the common man than ever before. As I view it, the Star of Bethlehem, symbolizing democracy and brotherly love, has so lighted the firmament that the oppressed and down-trodden of all nations can catch a glimpse of it and in God's appointed time will find a pathway to a nobler life. When fate shall take up its pen to write my final decree, I entertain the lively hope that a gracious Providence will dictate, "He fought a good fight, he kept the faith."

Index

Adams, Judge Spencer B., anecdote, 79
Agricultural and Technical College for Negroes, established in Greensboro, 45
Allen, Judge W. R., 78
Allen & Ginter, Richmond, Va., 194
American Insurance Company, Newark, 100
American Tobacco Company, in 1898 campaign, 52; mentioned, 189
American Tobacco Trust, 115, 116-17, 189
Anderson, Colonel, in Blackburn case, 107
Andrews, Colonel A. B., head of the Southern Railroad, 52, 61, 74 ff.
Andrews, Dan, during court week, 22-23
Armfield, Bill, 166
Armfield, Jess, defense of, 163 ff.
Atlantic Coast Line Railroad, 61

Babcock, Mary Reynolds, 154-55, 158
Badger game, 125-26
Bagley, Nancy Reynolds, 154-55, 158
Bailey, Josiah W., in 1898 campaign, 52; defeats Simmons for Senate, 135
Baker, Newton D., 91
Barnett, Tom, and a fox hunt, 8
Barringer, Colonel John A., 47, 79
Barstow & Company, 118
Bell, Dr., and the Matthews case, 67
Benbow, Dr. Evan, 46
Bennett College, Greensboro, chartered, 45
Bethel Hill Academy, 12
Black, Hugh, 142
Blackburn, Spence, 106-7
Blackwell, W. T., 192-93
Bogert on Trusts and Trustees, 174-75
Bonsack, James A., 193-94
Boone, R. B., in Lunsford case, 23; nominated solicitor, 49-50; in *State* v. *Murray,* 54
Bowie, Thomas C. ("Tam"), 137
Boyd & Brooks, 34-36

Boyd, James E., characterized, 34, 36 ff.; anecdotes, 36 ff.; mentioned, 47, 107
Brights, the, 146
Bright tobacco, secret of, 188, 190
Brim, Kenneth M., 39
Brooks, Ann, grandmother of A. L. B., 4
Brooks, Aubrey Lee, ancestry and birth of, 1 ff.; boyhood of, 6 ff., 10ff.; effect of war's aftermath upon, 13; early school days of, 12-13; teaches school, 17; receives law degree from the University of North Carolina, 18, 200-1; practices law in Roxboro, 18 ff.; influenced by W. W. Kitchin, 18-20; puts Kitchin in nomination for Congress, 29; campaigns with Kitchin, 30; marries Miss Maud Harris, 33; moves to Greensboro and enters partnership with James E. Boyd, 34 ff.; in case of Postal Telegraph Company, 35-36; attitude of toward Republicans, 38-39; nominated for solicitor in ninth judicial district, 50; elected, 52; experiences of as prosecuting attorney, 53 ff.; antagonizes Simmons, 59 ff.; antagonizes railroad interests, 61-62; manages Stedman's campaign for governor in 1904, 74 ff.; death of wife of, 62-63; resigns as solicitor after ten years, 78 ff.; rejects R. J. Reynolds' invitation to become chief counsel, 90; announces candidacy to succeed W. W. Kitchin in Congress, 83; loses, 84 ff.; camping trip in sandhill country, 88 ff.; turns to the law, 90, 92 ff.; marries Miss Helen Higbie, 92-93; builds home in Irving Park, Greensboro, 93; joins First Presbyterian Church, 94; adds a lake to "a lady, a library," 93-94; active in life insurance development of Greensboro, 96 ff.; in post office robbery case, 107 ff.; conducts case against James B. Duke and

209

Brooks, Aubrey Lee, (cont'd)
his Power Company, 113 ff.; for the defense in the Cole case, 127; makes keynote address at 1928 state convention, 133-34; breaks with management of Jefferson Standard, 136; recommended to vacancy on U. S. Supreme Court, 137; visits Franklin D. Roosevelt at Warm Springs, Ga., 137; correspondence of with F. D. R. quoted, 138 ff.; belief of in Roosevelt and New Deal, 142; travels of, 143 ff.; in Cannon-Reynolds-Holman case, 149 ff.; in Lassiter case and others, 160 ff.; as trustee of the First Presbyterian Church in the Richardson will case, 167 ff. *passim;* close connection of with tobacco industry in all stages, 188-89; on Jefferson and Lincoln, 196 ff.; on retirement, 203 ff.; on "the law's final decree," 207

Brooks, Aubrey Lee, son of A. L. B., 93
Brooks, Chestina Hall, mother of A. L. B., 5, 12; insists on her son's education, 16 ff.
Brooks, Helen Higbie (Mrs. Aubrey Lee Brooks), marriage of, 92; the lady of the lake, 93-94; travels of, 143 ff.
Brooks, James Taylor, son of A. L. B., 93
Brooks, Larkin, grandfather of A. L. B., 2, 12, 13
Brooks, Robert, son of A. L. B., 63
Brooks, Thornton Higbie, son of A. L. B., 93; member of firm, 102
Brooks, Dr. Zachary Taylor, father of A. L. B., 4-5, 12, 16 ff., 66; paper writing of wins case, 123 ff.
Brooks, McLendon & Holderness, 173
Brooks, McLendon, Brim & Holderness, 102
Brown, Judge George H., 78
Bruces, the, of Virginia, 14
Brummitt, Attorney General Dennis G., 133
Bryan, William Jennings, 30, 31, 61, 85, 200
Bryant, Victor S., in Lunsford case, 23; in *State* v. *Murray,* 54; nominates Stedman, 77
Bull Durham, effect of Civil War on popularity of, 192; story of brand name of, 192
Bull Durham Company, war of with Dukes, 194

Burley tobacco, substitute for Turkish, 194
Burlington Mills, 48
Busbee, F. H., 61
Bush, Harry R., 100
Butler, Marion, U. S. Senator, 59
Buxton, Cameron, 83
Bynum, W. P., in Lunsford case, 23, 24; as solicitor for State, 25-26; anecdotes, 80; and Duke Power Company case, 117; in Taylor case, 122; mentioned, 47, 126
Byrd, William, II, and boundary line, 1

Cabarrus Bank and Trust Company, and Cannon-Reynolds-Holman case, 152 ff. *passim*
Caldwell, David, 40 ff.
Caldwell, Thomas, son of David, 43, 44
Caldwell Institute, 44
Camel cigarettes, 194-95
Campaign of 1896, 28 ff.
Campaign of 1898, 49 ff.
Campaign of 1900, 59 ff.
Campaign of 1908, 82 ff.
Campaign of 1928, 132 ff.
Campaign of 1932, 136 ff.
Camp Bragg, selection of site for, 91
Cannon, Anne. *See* Reynolds, Anne Cannon
Cannon, Annie L., wife of Joe Cannon, 152 ff.
Cannon, Charles, Cabarrus Bank and Trust Company, 152-53
Cannon, J. W., founder of Cannon Mills, grandfather of Anne Cannon, 149
Cannon, Joe, father of Anne Cannon, 148 ff. *passim*
Cannon, Joseph G., congressman, 106-7
Cannon-Reynolds-Holman case, 149 ff.
Cansler, Edward T., 117, 137
Cape Fear and Yadkin Valley Railroad, 46
Cardozo, Benjamin, 138
Carlson, Mrs. C. I., 168
Carr, Julian S., 59 ff.
Carruthers, Eli, 45
Chapin, Mrs. Chester, 168
Cigarette industry, development of, 188 ff.
Clark, Walter, and the 1896 campaign, 31; as judicial statesman, 61; biography of, by A. L. B., 202; mentioned, 200
Cleveland, Grover, 28
Coble, Judge, in Lunsford case, 24

Cole case, the, 127 ff.
Coler, Bird, 113
Coler, W. N., 113 ff. *passim*
Cone Export and Commission Company, 48
Cone Memorial Hospital, 47
Cone, Moses, 47
"Coquette," drama based on Cole case, 127
Covington, H. H., 201
Cowles, Henry Clay, anecdote, 37
Craig, Locke, 85 ff.
Cummings, Homer, 138

Daniels, Josephus, active in Roosevelt's 1932 campaign, 138 ff. *passim;* mentioned, 200
Danville, Va., tobacco market, 189
Davidson College, 171, 179
Davis, John W., 117, 132, 144
Devin, W. A., 201
Dick, Robert P., 46, 47
Dillard, John H., 46
Dixie Fire Insurance Company, 92, 97-98, 100, 101
Douglas, Martin, 46
Douglas, Robert D., 46
Douglas, Robert M., member of State Supreme Court, 46
Douglas, Stephen A., 46
Duke, Benjamin, 193
Duke, Brodie, 193
Duke, James B. ("Buck"), 113, 115, 193
Duke, Washington, 193
Duke Power Company, 138. *See also North Carolina Public Service Company v. Duke Power Company*
Duke (W.) Sons and Company, 193-94
Dukes, the, 52, 193, 194
Durham, N. C., 191 ff.
Durham Bull Tobacco Company, 189

Edgeworth Female Academy, 44
Everett, Judge Willis M., 172 ff. *passim*

Faulkners, the, of Virginia, 14
Ferguson, Judge G. S., 78
Findley, Judge, in Cole case, 127
First Presbyterian Church, Greensboro, organized, 43; and the Lunsford Richardson will, 167 ff.
Fisher v. Water Company, 64
Fishing, as pastime, 204-5
Foushee, Howard, 200

Fowle, Daniel G., 74
Fox hunting, in Person County, 6 ff.; in Sandhills, 88 ff.
Frazier & Frazier, 176
Fuller, Jones, in *State* v. *Murray,* 54, 56
Fuller, Colonel Thomas, anecdote, 84-85
Fusion, of Populists and Republicans, 28; defeated Democrats 1896, 49; defeated 1898, 51 ff.

Gardner, O. Max, 135, 138
Gardners, the, of Virginia, 14
Garrett, Paul, and gold brick case, 70 ff.
Gattis v. *Kilgo,* 32
Gentry, Tom, schoolmate of A. L. B., 13
Gilmer, John A., 46
Glenn, R. B., 74 ff.
Glenns, the, of Virginia, 14
Goff, Judge Guy D., 107
Gold, P. D. and Charles, 98
Gold brick case, 70 ff.
Gorrell v. *Water Company,* 64 ff.
Graham, Judge W. A., 57
Grant, President U. S., 46
Gray, Julius A., 46
Green, John Ruffin, 191-92
Green, Squire, 191
Greene, General Nathanael, 40
Greensboro, attractive place to practice law, 33-34; the story of, 40 ff.; as Hartford of the South, 96 ff.
Greensboro Academy, chartered, 44
Greensboro Chamber of Commerce, 201-2
Greensboro Country Club, 97
Greensboro Daily News, 139
Greensboro Golf Club, 201
Greensboro Life Insurance Company, 98
Gretter, John A., 45
Grimsley, George A., 98, 171
Guilford College, influence of, 43
Guilford County, beginnings of, 40 ff.
Guilford Court House, 40
Guthrie, W. A., in Matthews case, 67
Guthrie, W. B., in *State* v. *Murray,* 54

Hall, Andrew, grandfather of A. L. B., 2-4, 13
Hamilton, Alexander, 199
Hanes, P. H., 98
Harriman, E. H., 52
Harris, Miss Maud (Mrs. Aubrey Lee Brooks), marriage of, 33; death of, 62-63
Harrises, the, of Virginia, 14

211

Harrison, Carter H., and the gold brick case, 72-73
Hayes, Helen, played leading role in "Coquette," based on Cole case, 127
Hayes, Judge Johnson J., partner of A. L. B., 38; recommends A. L. B. for U. S. Supreme Court, 137; and Richardson will case, 176-77, 178, 184-85; mentioned, 160
Hayne, Robert Y., 54
Higbie, Miss Helen. *See* Brooks, Helen Higbie
Hill, John, Negro boy chum of A. L. B., 7, 9
Hines, Richard K., 176
Hoey, Clyde R., 134
Hoke, Judge William A., 78
Holderness, George A., 102
Holderness, Howard, 103
Holderness, W. H., 102
Hole, Charles, 115
Hole Brothers, New York, 113 ff. *passim*
Holman, Libby, Smith Reynolds' second wife, 151 ff. *passim*
Holmes, Judge Oliver Wendell, quoted, 117
Holt, J. Allen, 83, 84
Holton, A. E., 107, 109
Hooker, Richard, quoted on the law, 207
Hoover, Herbert, 132, 133
Horner brothers, 12
Hull, Cordell, 133
Hunt, Nathan, 45
Hunting, 205-6. *See also* Fox hunting
Hunts, the, of Virginia, 14

Jackson, Andrew, 43, 200
Jackson, Thomas J., 120
Jarvis, Thomas J., 90
Jefferson, Thomas, in education of A. L. B., 196; Lincoln's letter on quoted, 197-99; mentioned, 61, 199
Jefferson Standard Life Insurance Company, 98-99, 101-3
Johnston, General Joseph E., 13, 192, 199
Jordan, J. F., 70, 88 ff.

Kernersville post office robbery, 107 ff.
Kilgo, Dr. John C., 32, 52
King, H. S., 176
King, R. R., Sr., 171 ff. *passim*
King, R. R., Jr., 176
Kitchin, Claude, in Congress, 82-83; mentioned, 19, 200

Kitchin, William H., member of Congress, father of W. W. Kitchin, 19, 29
Kitchin, W. W., influence of on A. L. B., 18-20; in Lunsford case, 23 ff.; in 1896 campaign, 29-30, 31, 49; in 1908 campaign, 82, 83 ff.; mentioned, 197, 200
Koerner, J. G., 192

Lansdale, Mr., anecdotes, 27
Lash, Dr. W. A., 46
Lassiter case, 160 ff.
Latham, J. E., 98
"Law's final decree," 207-8
Lee, General Robert E., statue of at Lexington, Virginia, 120-21, 139
Lefler, Hugh Talmage, aids in editing *The Papers of Walter Clark*, 202
Liggett & Myers, 189
Lincoln, Abraham, and John A. Gilmer, 46; letter of on Jefferson quoted, 197-99; mentioned, 200
Lindabury, Richard V., 117
Lindley, J. Van, 98
Lingle, Walter, 182
"Log College," Caldwell's, 41-42
Long, Judge B. F., 164 ff. *passim*, 78
Lorillard Company, 189
Lunsford, Nathan, trial of, 23-26
Lutherans, in North Carolina, 41

McAlister, A. W., 97
Macay, Judge Spruce, and David Caldwell, 42-43
McCanless & Early, 176
McIntosh, Colonel, 35
McLean, Angus W., 133 ff. *passim*, 134-35, 137
McNinch, Frank, 134
Macy, Everit, 91
Manly, Henderson & Womble, 176
Manning, Judge John, 200
Manning, J. S., in *State* v. *Murray*, 54
Martin, Governor Alexander, 40
Martin, Miss Martha, 46
Martinsville, Guilford County, 40
Matthews, Dr., trial of for murder, 66-68
Max, Abe, and Judge Winston, 56-57
Maxwell, A. J., 119
Mendenhall, Dr. Nereus, 43, 45
Merritt, J. S., 23
Michaud et al v. *Girod et al*, 174, 175
Moore, Judge Fred, 78
Moore, Larry, 201

Morehead, Colonel James T., 47
Morehead, Governor John M., 44, 46
Morehead, John Motley, in 1908 campaign, 84
Morrison, Cameron, 134, 135

Neal, Gabriel, 23
Negroes, in Greensboro, four of twelve members establishing the First Presbyterian Church, 43, 45; education of, 45; rights of, 45
Newton, Squire, 18
North Carolina, progress of, 202
North Carolina Bar Association, 202
North Carolina Public Service Company v. Duke Power Company, 113 ff.
North State Fire Insurance Company, 92, 97, 98

Old Bright Tobacco Belt, 188 ff.
Ormond, Bill, deceased in Cole case, 127 ff.
Osborne, Colonel W. H., 75, 84-85
Osborne, Judge, 117
"Overhills," and Camp Bragg, 90-91
Overman, Lee S., 60, 135
Owenses, the, of Virginia, 14

Page Railroad, 61
Paisley, Rev. William D., 44, 45
Parker, Captain E. S., 90, 102
Pass-Toters' victory, 74 ff.
Person County, and the War Between the States, 13; importance of in Old Bright Tobacco Belt, 190-91
Peebles, Judge R. B., anecdote, 36-37; in *State v. Murray*, 54, 55; mentioned, 78
Pilot Life Insurance Company, 97, 101
"Poplar Hall," home of A. L. B., 93
Populist party, 28. *See also* Fusion
Porter Drug Store (Greensboro), 47
Porter, William Sydney (O. Henry), 47
Postal Telegraph Company, 92
Post office robbery, Kernersville, 107 ff.
Presbyterians, in North Carolina, 41, 43
Presbyterian Church in the United States, General Assembly of, and Richardson will case, 180 ff.
Preyer, Mrs. W. Y., 168
Price, Captain Charles, 61-62
Price, Ralph, 103
Polikoff and Graves, 154
Politics, in Fifth District (N. C.), 28 ff. *See also* Campaigns

Quakers, in piedmont North Carolina, 43

Ragland, Major R. L., 191
Ragland brothers, and Lassiter case, 161 ff.
Railroads, in Greensboro, 46; political power of, 51-52, 61-62
Raper, Emery, in Armfield case, 165
Raskob, John J., and 1928 campaign, 134
Reams, Henry A., 193
Red shirt campaign, 51
Reid, Reuben D., 83
Retirement, A. L. B. on, 203-6
"Reynolda," home of Smith Reynolds, 150
Reynolds, Anne Cannon, 149 ff. *passim*
Reynolds, R. J., founder of Reynolds Tobacco Company, 90, 194-95
Reynolds, Richard J., 154-55, 158
Reynolds, W. N., 152, 194
Reynolds, Zachary Smith, 148 ff. *passim*
Reynolds Tobacco Company, 90, 189, 193-94
Richardson, H. Smith, 167 ff. *passim*
Richardson, Lunsford, Sr., will of, 167 ff.
Richardson, Lunsford, Jr., 167 ff. *passim*
Richardson, Mary Lynn, 168 ff. *passim*
Richardson, R. P., 98
Rink, Reuben. *See* Koerner, J. G.
Robinson, R. M., 176
Robinson, W. S. O'B., 117
Rockefeller, Percy, 90-91
Roosevelt, Mrs. Eleanor, 136
Roosevelt, Franklin D., and campaign of 1932 in North Carolina, 136 ff.; quotations from letters of, 138 ff.; mentioned, 132, 200
Roosevelt, Theodore, 52, 106
Rose, Charles G., 173
Roxboro, Brooks family move to, 9, 17; A. L. B.'s law practice in, 18 ff.; court week, 21
Royster, General, 83
Ruffin, Thomas, anecdote, 79; mentioned, 191
Russell, Governor Daniel L., 50
Russia, visited in 1936, 146-47

Schenck, Judge David, 47
Scott, Professor Austin, 179-80
Scott, J. W., 98
Seaboard Air Line, 61
Security Life and Annuity Company, 98, 162 ff.

213

Security Life and Trust Company, 98-99
Sedgefield, opened, 97
Settle, Justice Thomas, 29, 46
Settle, Thomas, 2nd, 28, 29-30, 82
Shaw, Leslie M., 104 ff.
Shaw, Thomas J., 49
Shenandoah Valley, 120 ff., 139
Shepherd, Chief Justice James E., 200, 201
Sherman, General William T., 13, 192, 199
Shuping, C. L., 141
Simmons, F. M., in White Supremacy campaign, 50; in 1898 campaign, 51-52; in campaign of 1900, 59; in 1928 campaign, 133 ff. *passim*
Simmons machine, 61
Slade brothers, 190
Smith, Alfred E., 132, 133 ff. *passim*
Smith, Dr. Henry Louis, 182
Smith, Jacob Henry, 45, 169
Smith, Marion W., 176
Southern Railway, 36, 74 ff.
Staples, Colonel, 47
State College, Raleigh, 52
State Corporation Commission, 118-19
State Penitentiary, 50
State v. Murray, 53 ff.
Stedman, Charles M., 67, 74 ff.
Stephens (J. F.) Company, 48
Sterling, Professor Richard, 44
Stevens, Thaddeus, 199
Strickland, Judge, in Taylor case, 122
Strike suit, 68-69
Strudwick, Judge, 117, 126

Taft, William Howard, 85, 117
Taylor, C. C., 98
Taylor, Dr., defense of, 122 ff.
Thompson, Judge Seymour, 65
Tobacco, effect of Civil War on popularity of, 191; discovery of bright, 188, 190; use of burley, 194
Tourgée, Judge Albion W., anecdote, 79-80
Travels, to France, Germany, Italy, England, 144; Mediterranean cruise, Athens, Constantinople, Palestine, Jerusalem, Egypt, Naples, Rome, 145; Canada, Alaska, West Indies, Mexico, Russia, 146; Scandinavian countries, 147-48; Hawaiian Islands, Yosemite, 148

Treadway, Dr., classmate of Dr. Zachary Taylor Brooks, 121
Trinity College, 32
Turkish tobacco, 193, 194-95
Turner, Dr., 66

University of North Carolina, granted honorary degree to David Caldwell, 42; political and religious alliance against in 1898 campaign, 52; Law School of, 200-1
University of North Carolina Press, published A. L. B.'s *Walter Clark, Fighting Judge* and *The Papers of Walter Clark*, 202

Vance, Zebulon Baird, 29
Vaughn, R. G., 171 ff. *passim*
Vick Chemical Company, 48, 167 ff.

Wake Forest College, 158
Walker, Alexander, 193
Ward, Artemus, quoted on retirement, 204
Ward, Hallett, 201
Warlick, Judge, and the Cannon-Reynolds-Holman case, 153
Watson, Cyrus B., 31-32
Watts, George W., 193
Webb, Judge James, in Taylor case, 124-25
Webb, E. Y., 200-1
Webster, Daniel, quoted, 54
Webster, Colonel John R., quoted, 202
Western Union Telegraph Company, 36
Wharton, C. R., in Richardson will case, 176
Whedbee, Harry, 200
White supremacy campaign, 51 ff.
Wiley, Calvin H., 44
Williams, Clay S., 189
Wilson, Woodrow, 61, 200
Winstead, Charles S., 18, 34, 38
Winston, ex-Judge Robert W., 54-56
Wolfe, Squire, 72-73, 79
Womack, Judge T. B., 60
Woman's College of the University of North Carolina (State Normal and Industrial School), 44-45, 52

Zachary Smith Reynolds Foundation, 152-53

www.ingramcontent.com/pod-product-compliance
Lightning Source LLC
Chambersburg PA
CBHW021404290426
44108CB00010B/374